The
Fertility Revolution

The Fertility Revolution
A Supply-Demand Analysis

Richard A. Easterlin
and Eileen M. Crimmins

The University of Chicago Press
Chicago and London

Richard A. Easterlin is professor of economics at the University of Southern California and editor of *Population and Economic Change in Developing Countries*. Eileen M. Crimmins is assistant professor of gerontology at the University of Southern California.

The University of Chicago Press, Chicago 60637
The University of Chicago Press, Ltd., London

© 1985 by The University of Chicago

94 93 92 91 90 89 88 87 86 85   5 4 3 2 1

Library of Congress Cataloging in Publication Data

Easterlin, Richard Ainley, 1926–
   The fertility revolution.

   Bibliography: p.
   Includes index.
   1. Fertility, Human—Developing countries.
2. Fertility, Human—Developing countries—Case
studies.   3. Family size—Developing countries.
I. Crimmins, Eileen M.   II. Title.
HB1108.E24   1985   304.6′32′091724   85-1163
ISBN 0-226-18029-8

To the memory of
John D. Durand and Dorothy S. Thomas

Contents

Figures

Tables

Preface

The reasons for persisting high fertility in the Third World and the determinants of long-term fertility decline remain one of the foremost challenges to social science. Among the attempts at explanation is what has come to be called the "supply-demand" theory of fertility determination. Recently this theory was used as an organizing framework by an interdisciplinary National Academy of Sciences panel in a comprehensive review of the literature on fertility determinants in developing countries (Bulatao and Lee 1983). Empirical research to test this theory has, however, been lacking. This volume is an attempt to fill this gap through empirical tests reported in chapters 3 through 6.

This work grows out of research in which the authors have been engaged since the late seventies, sometimes in collaboration with others. Although earlier reports have been published, the present volume is new. Chapters 3 and 4 present a new analysis based on more rigorous and sophisticated techniques of the authors' World Fertility Survey report (Easterlin and Crimmins 1982). Chapters 5 and 6 comprise a rewriting and expansion in empirical content of two papers co-authored with two Indian colleagues, K. Srinivasan, director of the International Institute of Population Studies, Bombay, and Shireen J. Jejeebhoy, director of research, Family Planning Association of India, Bombay. One of these papers appeared in *Economic Development and Cultural Change* (vol. 32, no. 2 [January 1984], pp. 227–53; © 1984 by The University of Chicago Press) and the other in *Population and Development Review* (vol. 10, no. 2 [June 1984], pp. 273–96). We are grateful to the editors of the two journals for permission to republish these articles, as revised. We wish also to express our appreciation to Academic Press for permission to republish here in chapter 2 parts of chapter 15 in R. A. Bulatao and R. D. Lee (eds.), *Determinants of Fertility in Developing Countries*, vol. 2 (1983), pp. 562–86.

Most of the work reported here was conducted at the California Institute of Technology, University of Pennsylvania, and University of Southern California. Although we cannot fully acknowledge our many intellectual debts, some must be specifically mentioned. Most important is our debt to our collaborators, Srinivasan and Jejeebhoy; to David M. Grether, who advised on the econometric methods in chapters 3 and 4; to our principal research assistant on the material in this volume, Ramesh Amatya; and to our typist, Donna Hokoda, who set new standards of excellent and willing performance. For his continued interest, support, and encouragement under trying circumstances we are grateful to the late V. C. Chidambaram, who was at the time deputy project director, World Fertility Survey, London. We have especially benefited from many valuable comments and criticisms on the first draft of this study by Dennis Ahlburg, Susan Hill Cochrane, Allen C. Kelley, Warren Sanderson, and Morton Owen Schapiro.

At earlier stages this work benefited from discussions of theory and methods with Lance E. Davis, Mahmoud S. A. Issa, James Kocher, Robert A. Pollak, T. Paul Schultz, Robert Summers, Michael L. Wachter, the members of the National Academy of Sciences panel mentioned above, and participants in a 1981 University of Pennsylvania fertility research seminar that we conducted; from research assistance by Karen Fox, John McHenry, Mahesh Naik, and John Nye; and from typing assistance by Linda Benjamin, Adele Burns, and Sharon Koga. The index was prepared by Diane J. Macunovich.

The primary data used in the analysis of chapters 3 and 4 came from the fertility surveys in Colombia and Sri Lanka carried out within the World Fertility Survey programme. We wish to thank Mr. W. A. A. S. Peiris, director, Department of Census and Statistics, Government of Sri Lanka. The Colombian National Fertility Survey was conducted in 1976 jointly by the Corporación Centro Regional de Población (CCRP), a nonprofit private institution devoted to research on population, and the Departmento Administrativo Nacional de Estadística (DANE), the state agency responsible for the collection, processing, and publication of statistical data, with the collaboration of the Division of Information Systems of the Ministry of Health in the design and implementation of the sample. The cooperation of all these organizations is gratefully acknowledged.

Financial support for early work on chapters 3 and 4 was provided by the World Fertility Survey and the National Academy of Sciences, the latter under a grant from AID. Support for Richard A. Easterlin's participation in 1980–81 was also provided by the Sherman Fairchild Foundation at the California Institute of Technology. The research in chapters 5 and 6 grew out of a trip to India by the authors in December 1979–January 1980 made possible by the Ford Foundation, and was subsequently supported in part by Ford-Rockefeller Grant RF 77065, Allocation 165. Finally, we are indebted to our colleagues at the University of Southern California for many helpful comments and to the university for financial support.

I
The Problem and Approach

1
The Fertility Revolution

Throughout the world a shift from high to low fertility has invariably accompanied economic and social modernization. This change has largely been accomplished by family size limitation within marriage—by a shift from what is commonly called a natural fertility regime to one of deliberate control of family size by individual couples. This change in reproductive behavior is undoubtedly the most dramatic in human history and merits the designation "fertility revolution." Yet its causes remain unknown. Although the fertility revolution is associated in a general way with modernization, careful study of different countries reveals wide variability in their experience. Because of inadequate knowledge of the causes of the fertility revolution, it is not possible to predict the onset and pace of fertility decline in today's developing countries or to formulate effective policies to slow population growth.

The primary aim of this study is to test a theory of the causes of the fertility revolution. This chapter first presents a schematic view of the fertility revolution—the object of explanation. It then sketches the main ideas of the theory and indicates the nature of the empirical tests and subsequent organization of the volume.

The Nature of the Fertility Revolution

The fertility revolution is part of a much broader transformation, commonly termed "modernization," observed in a growing number of nations since the mid-eighteenth century (Coleman 1968; Easterlin 1968; Kuznets 1966; Lerner 1968; Inkeles and Smith 1974). On the economic side modernization involves a sustained rise in real output per head and wide-ranging changes in techniques of producing, trans-

3

porting, and distributing goods, in the scale and organization of productive activities, and in types of outputs and inputs. It also embraces
major shifts in the industrial, occupational, and spatial distribution of
productive resources and in the degree of exchange and monetization
of the economy. On the social and demographic side, it involves
significant alterations in fertility, mortality, and migration, in place of
residence, in family size and structure, in the educational system, and
in provision for public health. Its influence extends into the areas of
income distribution, class structure, government organization, and
political structure. In terms of human personality, modernization is
characterized by an increased openness to new experience, increased
independence from parental authority, belief in the efficacy of science,
and ambition for oneself and one's children.

Elements of this transformation are apparent in parts of northwestern Europe in the eighteenth century. In the course of the nineteenth
century, as modernization gathered increasing headway in its areas of
origin, it gradually diffused southward and eastward throughout
Europe. By the end of the century, its beginnings can be identified in
easternmost Europe, including Russia, and also in Japan. A somewhat
similar development was taking place concurrently in overseas areas
settled by Europeans, mirroring to some extent the diffusion pattern
within Europe. Modernization is apparent first in areas initially settled
chiefly by migrants from northwestern Europe—the United States in
the first part of the nineteenth century, followed by Canada, Australia,
and New Zealand—and subsequently in parts of Latin America,
where migration from southern and eastern Europe is especially important. In the twentieth century, and increasingly since World War
II, the initial signs of modernization have become more widespread in
parts of Asia and northern Africa and, more recently, in sub-Saharan
Africa.

The principal changes in reproductive behavior associated with
modernization relate to fertility and fertility control. The change in
fertility is from an average of six or more births per woman over the
reproductive career to around two. In terms of the crude birth rate, the
change is from magnitudes often of 40 per thousand or more to under
20. This shift in fertility from high to low levels, together with a similar
(and usually prior) decline in mortality, is termed "the demographic
transition." Viewed against the long backdrop of prior human experience, the magnitude of these changes is remarkable indeed. As regards fertility this point is made vividly by a commentator on the
English fertility decline:

The typical working class mother of the 1890's, married in her teens or early twenties and experiencing ten pregnancies, spent about fifteen years in a state of pregnancy and in nursing a child for the first years of its life. She was tied, for this period of time, to the wheel of childbearing. Today, for the typical mother, the time so spent would be about four years. A reduction of such magnitude in only two generations in the time devoted to childbearing represents nothing less than a revolutionary enlargement of freedom for women. (Titmuss 1966, p. 91)

The second feature of the fertility revolution is a shift in what some call the mode of fertility regulation—a shift from a situation in which fertility is controlled through various social and biological mechanisms to one of limitation of family size by the conscious decisions of individual households. The view is well expressed by the noted French demographer Bourgeois-Pichat (1967b, p. 163):

Fertility in preindustrialized societies seems to be strongly determined if not controlled in the sense we give to this word today. It is determined by a network of sociological and biological factors and when the network is known, the result can be predicted. Freedom of choice by couples is almost absent. The couples have the number of children that biology and society decide to give them.
One of the main features of the so-called demographic revolution has been precisely to change not only the level of fertility but also change its nature. Having a child has been becoming more and more the result of free decision of the couple. And this change in the nature of fertility may be more important than the change in its magnitude. Fertility has left the biological and social field to become part of the behavioural science. . . .
For fertility we had for a long while a lot of customs carefully molded in the course of time which almost completely determined the size of families. These customs are still there but they are for the most part useless, as fertility is now under the will of people.

The evidence for the shift to deliberate fertility control is principally of two types. Survey data, in which households report explicitly on their use of fertility control, show that in most developing countries the proportion of reproductive age women reporting any use of fertility control is low, frequently less than 10 percent; in contrast, in developed countries, the corresponding percentage approaches 80 percent or more. Additional evidence comes from analyses of census or other data on observed age specific marital fertility rates, using a technique developed by Ansley Coale and James Trussell based on

Louis Henry's work (Coale and Trussell 1974). These studies too show the difference in deliberate control just noted; they also show that in the distant past of today's developed countries, control was as infrequent as in today's developing countries (Knodel 1977; Easterlin, Pollak, and Wachter 1980, pp. 104–10; Knodel and van de Walle 1979; Robinson 1983).

As the Bourgeois-Pichat quotation indicates, to some observers the change in the mode of fertility regulation is even more significant than the decline in fertility itself because of the fundamentally new attitudes implied by household decisions consciously to limit their fertility. It is noteworthy that the foremost empirical scholar of modernization, Alex Inkeles, identifies as first among "personal qualities which . . . may validly be described as fitting a reasonable theoretical conception of modern man [that of] openness to new experience, both with people and with new ways of doing things *such as attempting to control births*" (1969, italics added). But the dramatic decline in fertility itself is of major consequence, not least because it frees modern woman from what Titmuss eloquently calls "the wheel of childbearing." To describe these changes collectively as a "fertility revolution" is clearly justified, as, indeed, is suggested by use of the word revolution in each of the previous quotations.

The relationship between the two aspects of the fertility revolution—the shift from high to low fertility and the change from "natural fertility" to adoption of deliberate control by individual households—is brought out diagrammatically in figure 1.1. In the figure, the degree of modernization is measured along the horizontal axis. Following Sauvy (1961), one may define:

1. reproductive potential, P, as the number of children that 1,000 married women in the most favorable conditions would have during their reproductive career;
2. natural fertility, N, as the number of children per 1,000 married women during their reproductive career if no conscious effort were made to regulate fertility.

In any society at a given time, even though no conscious effort is made by individual families to limit fertility, actual fertility will fall short of reproductive potential because of physiological conditions limiting fertility, such as malnutrition, or because of cultural circumstances, such as breastfeeding practices or an intercourse taboo, which have the unintended effect of lowering fertility. It is now widely recognized, for example, that breastfeeding prolongs postpartum amenorrhea and

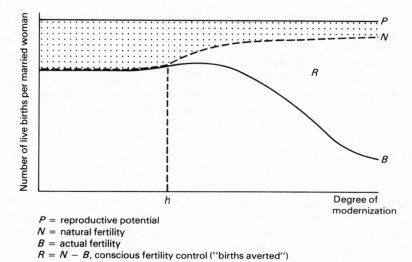

P = reproductive potential
N = natural fertility
B = actual fertility
R = N − B, conscious fertility control ("births averted")

Fig. 1.1 Schematic Representation of the Fertility Revolution

thus reduces fertility. Mothers breastfeed, however, not with a view to its fertility effect, of which they are apparently often unaware (see chap. 3 below), but because of its importance for the health and survival of the child. The fertility-suppressing effect is thus an unintended consequence of breastfeeding. Natural fertility, N, is therefore represented in figure 1.1 as lying below reproductive potential, P, the difference being due to conditions which from the point of view of the family unintentionally depress fertility. P is assumed in this diagram to remain constant throughout the course of modernization; natural fertility, N, to increase, as, say, the practice of breastfeeding diminishes with modernization (Bongaarts and Menken 1983).

The conditions envisioned in the Bourgeois-Pichat quotation imply that actual fertility, B, would be the same as natural fertility, N, in a premodern situation because there is no deliberate control of fertility by the individual family. This is depicted by the overlapping of B and N at the left side of the diagram. Fertility is, however, below the potential maximum because of cultural and physiological conditions inadvertently limiting births. At some point in the course of modernization, depicted here as h, actual fertility, B, begins to fall below natural fertility, N, as some households begin consciously to control fertility. To the right of point h, the vertical distance, R, between B and N, represents conscious fertility control, measured in terms of births averted. As the practice of deliberate family size limitation spreads, actual fertility, B, starts eventually to trend downward. As shown, there may be a period during which B rises, but this is not necessarily so. The diagram thus depicts a shift from premodern conditions, in which observed fertility corresponds to natural fertility, to modern conditions, where the spread of conscious fertility regulation is eventually associated with a downward trend in observed fertility.

The purpose of figure 1.1 is to give a schematic representation of the general trends in fertility and fertility control characterizing the fertility revolution. A more realistic picture would allow for the fact that marked fluctuations characterize fertility both in premodern and modern times, and especially in the former. One might allow, too, for the possibility of conscious fertility regulation among a limited segment of society even in premodern conditions, by allowing B to parallel N to the left of h, but at a lower level. Finally, the decline in fertility may be partly due to a concurrent change in nuptiality, a shift to a later age at marriage. This is particularly likely to be true of today's developing areas where age at marriage is sometimes quite low at the onset of modernization. Nevertheless, the principal long-term source of fertility decline is family size limitation within marriage. This is clear from the many empirical studies stimulated by Bongaarts' work (1978, 1982) partitioning reproductive potential along lines similar to those in figure 1.1. It follows that the adoption of family size limitation within marriage is the first priority in the explanation of the fertility revolution.

Causes of the Fertility Revolution

There are two popular explanations for high fertility and low use of deliberate fertility control in today's developing countries. One is lack of accessibility to family planning services and techniques. In this view what is needed to stimulate increased fertility control and lower fertility is increased public availability of family planning knowledge and services and/or new techniques of control, of which the pill and intrauterine device (IUD) are recent examples. The other explanation is lack of motivation; that is, parents in these countries want so many children that there is no incentive to limit family size.

Although both of these views identify potentially relevant considerations, neither suffices to explain actual experience. In the earlier history of the now-developed countries, there were no family planning programs or major innovations in fertility-control techniques. Yet these countries successfully accomplished the transition to deliberate control. As for desired family size, consider recent evidence for three countries to be analyzed more fully in this volume (data sources are given in table 7.1):

	Desired family size	Percent ever using fertility control
Colombia 1976	4.8	69
Sri Lanka 1975	4.6	56
India 1970	4.2	28

In all three of these countries, family size preferences are high, averaging between four and five children, and differ relatively little. Yet there is wide variation in the extent of fertility control, with control tending, if anything, to be highest in the country with the highest, not lowest, desired family size.

The theory of the present volume encompasses the explanations above but is not restricted to them. Family size desires correspond in the present theory to the "demand for children." Family planning accessibility is viewed as one element under the broader rubric, costs of fertility regulation—the easier the access to family planning services, the lower the costs faced by couples wishing to limit their fertility. In the present theory, however, "costs" also include subjective drawbacks of fertility control, such as distaste for the idea itself or for specific techniques like the IUD or induced abortion, as well as monetary costs. To these two factors—demand for children and regulation costs—the theory adds a third factor relating to the reproductive capacities of a couple, termed the "supply of children." The relevance of supply considerations, typically omitted from popular discussion and many scholarly theories, is illustrated by a modern couple that wants only two children but because of fecundity problems is unable to achieve its desires. For this couple, lack of fertility control stems, not from inordinately high family size desires or lack of access to fertility control techniques, but inadequate supply. In today's developing countries, an important limit on supply arises from high child mortality as well as fecundity limitations.

When supply is added to the picture, motivation for fertility control is no longer a matter merely of demand, but of the balance between supply and demand. As the illustration above shows, a couple may want only two children (its demand is low), but if it is unable to achieve that goal (its supply is even lower), there is no motivation for fertility control. Conversely, a couple that wants a large number of children (its demand is high) but with unregulated fertility is able to produce even more than it wants (its supply is even higher) will be motivated to limit its fertility so as to avoid unwanted children.

Focus of the Present Study

In general, then, in the present theory, a couple's use of fertility control is hypothesized to vary directly with the excess of their supply of children over demand—their motivation for fertility control—and inversely with their perceived costs of regulating fertility, subjective as well as objective. The most important single issue addressed here is whether, in fact, the evidence is consistent with this hypothesis. Thus, using recent data for Sri Lanka and Colombia, in chapters 3 and 4 we ask whether more use of fertility control characterizes households with higher motivation for control and/or lower costs of control. Chapters 5 and 6 explore a similar question with regard to geographic units rather than households; in chapter 5 we look at trends over time in rural and urban areas of the Indian state of Karnataka and the nation of Taiwan; in chapter 6 we look at differences among ten Indian states in 1970. In both chapters, we ask whether variations in use of control are associated in the expected way with motivation and regulation costs.

Note that, unlike popular views and a number of scholarly theories, the present approach does not assert the primacy of any single determinant of fertility control—motivation, its demand or supply components, or regulation costs. Rather it views the respective roles of these factors as an empirical issue, one to which the present volume seeks to contribute. Thus, assuming the relationships between use, motivation, and regulation costs are as hypothesized, the next question is how important in determining use is motivation versus regulation costs, and how important in determining motivation is demand versus supply? As above, these questions can be asked about variations among households (chaps. 3 and 4) or among geographic units, both over time and at a point in time (chaps. 5 and 6).

Also, assuming again that the theory holds, a number of substantive questions can be examined regarding the transition to deliberate control. For one, why is there so little use of control in a premodern society? Is it, perhaps, because of high regulation costs, for example, lack of knowledge of or access to family planning techniques as suggested by the "accessibility" theory? Or is it due to lack of motivation, that couples cannot achieve their family size desires even with unregulated fertility, that is, their supply is typically less than demand? Does the spread of deliberate control reflect growing motivation, declining regulation costs, or both? If motivation is growing, is it because of a declining demand for children, growing supply, or both? And what of the role of policy—what does the evidence suggest on the impact of family planning programs in accelerating the spread of control? Questions such as these are addressed throughout chapters 3 through 6. Also, since chapters 5 and 6 draw especially on the experience of India, they throw light on an important controversial issue, how successful India has been in accomplishing the transition to deliberate control.

As should be clear from the foregoing, the questions addressed here go directly to the heart of a major policy problem today—how to reduce fertility and population growth in today's developing countries. At one extreme are those who see family planning programs as the answer (i.e., lower costs of regulation); at the other are those who advocate socioeconomic development to increase motivation for fertility control. Our analysis provides a tentative basis for judging the relative merits of these views.

These, then, are the concerns of this study. The next chapter spells out the theoretical structure more fully, chapters 3 through 6 present the empirical studies, and chapter 7 summarizes and notes some research and policy implications.

2
Theoretical Framework

This chapter outlines the theoretical framework of this volume and the conceptual relations between modernization and fertility suggested by the theory. The origins of the theory go back to work by Tabarrah (1971), Wachter (1972), and Easterlin (1970, 1975); a similar approach was applied to contemporary American fertility behavior by Michael and Willis (1976). For a more detailed and formal exposition of the theory and fuller citation of relevant literature, see Easterlin (1978) and Easterlin, Pollak, and Wachter (1980).

The chapter begins by showing briefly how the present approach is related to previous empirical studies of the relation of modernization to fertility. It then describes the core variables of the framework—demand, supply, and regulation costs—and how they interact in determining fertility and fertility control behavior. Following this, the manner in which modernization influences fertility through this new set of variables is illustrated for several common features of modernization—advances in public health, schooling, urbanization, and the introduction of new goods and family planning programs. Finally, the relation of the present analysis to several well-known theories of the transition to low fertility is described.

Approaches to Studying the Impact of
Modernization on Fertility

Traditionally, a common approach to identifying links between modernization and fertility has been to regress fertility (as measured, say, by children ever born) on measures that reflect different aspects of modernization (see Richards 1983 for a brief survey). Sometimes other possible fertility determinants, such as cultural conditions, are

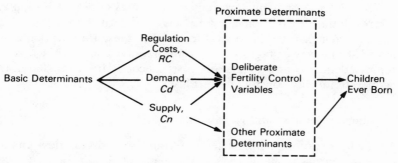

A. Multivariate Regression of Fertility on Basic Determinants

Basic Determinants ⎯⎯⎯⎯⎯⎯⎯⎯⎯⎯⎯⎯⎯→ Children Ever Born

B. Proximate Determinants Analysis

Basic Determinants ⎯⎯→ Proximate Determinants ⎯⎯→ Children Ever Born

C. Present Approach

Proximate Determinants

Basic Determinants

Regulation Costs, RC

Demand, Cd

Supply, Cn

Deliberate Fertility Control Variables

Other Proximate Determinants

Children Ever Born

Fig. 2.1 Approaches to Analyzing the Impact of Modernization on Fertility. Basic determinants include modernization variables (education, urbanization, etc.), cultural factors (ethnicity, religion, etc.), and other determinants such as genetic factors.

included in the regression. This approach is illustrated in panel A of figure 2.1.

The recent development of "proximate determinants" analysis (Davis and Blake 1956; Bongaarts 1978) has led to the insertion of a new stage in the sequence, so that now fertility is usually seen as determined directly by a set of "proximate determinants," with modernization, in turn, operating only indirectly on fertility through these determinants (see fig. 2.1, panel B; cf. also Bongaarts 1978, p. 106). The proximate determinants comprise factors such as extent of exposure to intercourse, fecundability (including frequency of intercourse), duration of postpartum infecundability, spontaneous intrauterine mortality, sterility, and use of deliberate fertility control (contraception and induced abortion).

The approach adopted here can be thought of as a further evolution of these two approaches. It singles out one subset of proximate determinants, that relating to deliberate fertility control, and inserts still another set of variables (supply, demand, and regulation costs) between deliberate control and modernization (panel C). As applied to the fertility transition, this approach thus sees the various modernization variables as impinging directly on supply (including the proximate determinants other than fertility control), demand, and costs of regulation. These three factors, in turn, shape the trend in use of deliberate control and fertility, through interactions explained below. The present approach can thus be thought of as a continuation of the theoretical trend started by proximate determinants analysis toward the introduction of new links between modernization and fertility.

The next section explains briefly the concepts of demand, supply, and regulation costs. Then, a few aspects of modernization are singled out and their possible impact on fertility via these three variables is traced through two stages—first, from the modernization factors to supply, demand, and regulation costs; second, from the latter to deliberate fertility control and fertility.

Demand, Supply, and Regulation Costs

The list of potential influences on fertility is almost limitless. In the present approach, all of the determinants of fertility are seen as working through one or more of the following three categories:

1. The demand for children, the number of surviving children parents would want if fertility regulation were costless. This depends on household tastes (including tastes relating to child "quality"), income, and child cost considerations, including both the economic and noneconomic returns from children as well as their costs. It is roughly approximated by survey responses on desired family size.
2. The supply of children, the number of surviving children a couple would have if they made no deliberate attempt to limit family size. This reflects both a couple's natural fertility and the chances of child survival. As has been noted, natural fertility and hence the supply of children may be well below the biological maximum because of cultural conditions such as prolonged breastfeeding that inadvertently reduce fertility.
3. The costs of fertility regulation. This lumps together a couple's attitudes toward and access to fertility control methods and supplies. It includes both subjective disadvantages of regulation such as distaste for the general notion of family planning and the drawbacks of specific techniques like abortion, and the eco-

nomic costs of control, such as the time and money required to procure family planning services.

The following discussion of demand, supply, and regulation costs is synoptic. For a comprehensive treatment including full reference to relevant literature, see Bulatao and Lee (1983).

Demand for children, Cd.—In keeping with the economic theory of household choice, the immediate determinants of the demand for children are income, prices, and tastes. Traditionally, these considerations have been emphasized in the "economics of fertility" (cf. Becker 1960, 1965; Leibenstein 1957, 1974; Schultz 1981; Willis 1974). The demand for children is seen as depending on the household's balancing of its subjective tastes for goods and children against externally determined constraints of price and income in a way that maximizes its satisfaction. Variations in the basic taste, price, and income determinants will cause differences in demand among households at a given time or for a given household over time. Other factors being constant, the number of children desired would be expected to vary directly with household income (assuming children are a "normal" good), directly with the price of goods relative to children, and inversely with the strength of tastes for goods relative to children. It is through tastes or subjective preferences that many attitudinal considerations stressed by sociologists operate, such as norms regarding family size and standards of child care and rearing.

The demand for children refers to children of a given quality, that is, children embodying a given set of inputs of time and goods. Allowance can be made for variations in child quality by viewing child quality as an additional good along with number of children and goods consumed by the parents. An increase in income would then be expected to raise both the number of children and the standard of child quality, whereas a rise in the relative prices of inputs required for children would lead to substitution against both child numbers and child quality. Also, subjective preferences relating to child quality might change, leading, for example, to greater emphasis by parents on the quality of children at the expense of number of children.

Potential supply of children, Cn.—On the production side of fertility determination, the key analytical concept is the potential supply of children—the number of surviving children a household would have if fertility were not deliberately limited. This depends, in turn, on natural fertility and the probability of a baby surviving to adulthood. Given natural fertility, an increase in infant and child survival prospects would increase the potential supply of children. Similarly, given survival prospects, the potential supply of children would vary directly with natural fertility.

The immediate determinants of natural fertility are (a) period of exposure to intercourse, (b) fecundability (including frequency of intercourse), (c) duration of postpartum infecundability, (d) spontaneous intrauterine mortality, and (e) sterility (cf. Bongaarts 1978, 1982). These factors, in turn, may depend partly on physiological or biological factors and partly on cultural practices. Biological factors would include those that influence natural fertility through such mechanisms as genetic effects on fecundity or the effect of disease and malnutrition on coital frequency and the ability to carry a fetus to term. Cultural factors would include various social customs or events that inadvertently affect coital frequency, fecundity, or fetal mortality. Natural fertility in a given society and the potential supply of children are likely to be below the reproductive potential of the population because of both biological constraints and cultural conditions that inadvertently reduce childbearing.

It is clear from this concept of natural fertility that the existence in a given society of a practice that reduces fertility below the physiological maximum is not in itself evidence that households are deliberately restricting fertility. The critical question is the meaning attached to the practice by its users. If, for example, abstinence is practiced by a couple as a way of limiting family size, then there is deliberate regulation of fertility. But if abstinence is due to observance of a taboo on intercourse while a mother is nursing, then there is no deliberate control, and the practice is simply one of various cultural conditions that keep natural fertility below the physiological maximum. In sociology the question of the intent behind a given social practice is formalized by distinguishing between the "manifest" and "latent" functions of the practice, corresponding roughly to the intended and unforeseen consequences. Allied notions in anthropology are the concepts of "emic" and "etic," which refer to the meaning attached to a phenomenon, by, respectively, the actors themselves and independent observers (Harris 1968, pp. 571–75).

From survey data on knowledge and use of deliberate fertility control, it is clear that family size concerns play an important part in decisions on contraception and induced abortion, but such concerns do not seem to enter significantly into decisions on age at marriage or length of breastfeeding, though in principle these too are among the options available to couples for limiting family size. In most empirical research, therefore, deliberate control has come to be identified with the practice of contraception or induced abortion and this is the concept adopted here (cf., e.g., Bongaarts 1978, Bongaarts and Menken 1983).

Motivation for fertility regulation, $Cn - Cd$.—The potential supply of and demand for children jointly determine the motivation for fertility regulation. If the potential supply falls short of demand ($Cn < Cd$), there is no desire to limit fertility; on the contrary, an "excess demand" situation of this type would result in a demand for ways to enhance fertility and for the adoption of children (although these possibilities are usually quantitatively unimportant). Households might have knowledge of the means of regulating fertility, but there would be no incentive to use them. In this situation, parents would be expected to have as many children as possible; that is, the number of children parents actually have would correspond to their potential supply. Variations in the number of surviving children parents have would arise from variations in the determinants of potential supply, namely, natural fertility and the probability of an infant surviving to adulthood.

On the other hand, if the potential supply exceeds demand ($Cn > Cd$)—an "excess supply" situation—parents would be faced with the prospect of having unwanted children and would be motivated to regulate their fertility. In an excess supply situation, therefore, there is a demand for ways of limiting fertility. The larger this excess, the greater is the potential burden of unwanted children, and consequently the greater is a household's motivation to limit its fertility. It is worth stressing the two-sided view here of how motivation for fertility control is determined, that is, by both demand and supply. Often motivation is simply identified with desired family size, that is, demand, and it is assumed that only if there are economic and social changes leading people to desire smaller families will deliberate fertility control be adopted. In fact, however, even if demand remains constant, an increase in supply can increase motivation and generate a need for fertility control. An increase in supply might arise from an increase in a couple's natural fertility, improved chances of child survival, or both.

Fertility regulation costs, RC.—Although motivation is a necessary condition for fertility regulation, it is not a sufficient condition. Fertility regulation imposes costs on the household of two types. There are psychic costs—the displeasure associated with the idea or practice of fertility control—and market costs—the time and money necessary to learn about and use specific techniques. These costs, in turn, depend upon (*a*) the attitudes in society toward the general notion of fertility control and toward specific techniques, and (*b*) the degree of access to fertility control, in terms of both the availability of information and the range of specific techniques and their prices. Typically, a family planning program lowers market costs by increasing information and providing services free or below cost. It also lowers subjective costs by lending legitimacy to the notion of practicing birth control.

Whether fertility control will actually be used in a given excess supply situation depends on how the costs of fertility regulation compare with the motivation to limit fertility. Given the strength of the motivation, the lower the costs of fertility regulation—that is, the more nearly conditions approach those of the "perfect contraceptive society," where psychic and market costs would be zero (Bumpass and Westoff 1970)—the greater would be the adoption of fertility regulation and the more nearly would the number of children parents have correspond to the number they desire. Conversely, the higher the costs of fertility control, the more nearly would actual conditions approach the potential supply of children, the lower would be the deliberate control of fertility, and the greater would be the number of unwanted children. If regulation costs are very high relative to motivation, then a couple may feel that the disadvantages of unwanted children are less than the disadvantages of the methods required for deliberately regulating its fertility, and hence forego fertility control. Again, natural fertility may be a rational response to the couple's basic situation. Recognition of the influence of regulation costs on adoption of fertility control explains why survey respondents may report that they want no more children (implying that they are "motivated"), and yet do nothing to prevent having them.

In sum, if the three central determinants (demand, supply, and regulation costs) do not result in deliberate family size limitation, then a couple's observed fertility will correspond to its natural fertility and depend on the circumstances governing its natural fertility—period of exposure, fecundability, duration of postpartum infecundability, fetal wastage, and sterility. If the determinants result in deliberate control then this enters along with the conditions just mentioned to determine observed fertility as in the usual proximate determinants analysis. Needless to say, the typical couple's decision whether or not to limit family size is viewed here not as a highly formal decision, but as a gradual response to the balance between these various types of pressures.

Some qualifications.—As with any theory a number of simplifying assumptions are made. As indicated, the theory assumes that age at marriage is largely exogenous to the decision on deliberate fertility control, that is, in deciding on when to marry couples are not significantly influenced by the potential effect on family size. The present view was put cogently by Ansley Coale (1975, p. 349): "Few couples marry at 25 instead of 24 because of a calculation that they will have one less birth; whereas the practice of contraception or induced abortion has as its direct object fewer births." It is illustrated by the findings of recent research on Thailand, where intensive interviews show that individuals "make little connection between age at marriage and the number of children eventually born" (Knodel, Havanon, and Pramualratana 1984, p. 317). Similarly, a study of South India reports:

> In an examination of a decade's marriages among a population of 5,000 persons, marriages largely characterized by brides marrying later than their mothers did, we did not find a single case of the marriage being explained or justified in terms of a smaller final family size, or even of young parents having fewer children on their hands while they were establishing themselves. Indeed, it is widely felt that a woman who marries two or three years after menarche will probably be more fecund because her reproductive powers will not be impaired by early damage. (Caldwell et al. 1983, p. 359)

It should be understood that the view adopted here is that age at marriage is not used deliberately to affect fertility. Certainly, age at marriage does have an impact on fertility, but this effect is largely inadvertent, like that of breastfeeding, and does not arise from attempts deliberately to limit family size. Nor is it intended to imply that research into nuptiality is unimportant. But to understand the fertility revolution, it is the determinants of deliberate control, chiefly contraception and induced abortion, that are most important.

As stated here, the theory focuses on use of deliberate control for limiting numbers of children and disregards the use of control for spacing. The theory could be expanded into a sequential decision-making model incorporating spacing by taking account of variations over the reproductive career in demand, supply, and regulation costs. Demand, for example, would then include a couple's desired spacing as well as numbers of children (Easterlin 1978, p. 128). But empirical implementation of such a scheme would be difficult; there are, for example, few data on spacing desires or that differentiate between use of control for spacing versus limiting numbers. More important, as the

United Nations (1981, p. 160) observes: "the factors affecting the motivation to delay and space births seem to be related to the factors affecting the motivation for birth limitation." In line with this, one may reasonably claim that the present theory captures important factors determining decisions on spacing as well as numbers of children. For example, other things equal, a couple that is more fecund, and thus has a high potential supply of children, would be more likely to feel pressures to start spacing children as well as limiting the number. Similarly, a couple with a low demand for children might be expected, other things constant, to start spacing children earlier as well as limiting numbers sooner. Given an alternative, then, between a cumbersome theory that would be difficult to implement empirically and one reasonably consonant with available data that bears on decisions about spacing as well as numbers, the choice was obvious.

Finally, we disregard sex preferences in the present analysis, though they too could be included. In part, this is because of the nature of our primary concern, it seems unlikely that changes in sex preferences have, as a general matter, been a prime mover behind the fertility revolution. In part, it is to simplify the analysis. Clearly attention to sex preferences and, data permitting, spacing per se would be useful extensions of the present work.

Links from Modernization to Supply, Demand, and Regulation Costs

As has been seen, the different aspects of modernization are seen as potentially affecting fertility via all three variables—demand, supply, and regulation costs. To illustrate this reasoning, five aspects of modernization are selected here:

1. innovations in public health and medical care,
2. innovations in formal schooling,
3. urbanization,
4. the introduction of new goods, and
5. the establishment of a family planning program.

As is clear from the earlier description of modernization, these aspects are far from exhaustive. There are many other obvious candidates for inclusion such as per capita income growth, female employment in the modern sector, changes in family structure, mass media developments, modernization of government administration, and changes in human attitudes and personality, to mention only a few.

Table 2.1 Direction of Effect of Various Aspects of Modernization on Indicated Determinants of Deliberate Fertility Control

Aspect of modernization	(1) Tastes	(2) In-come	(3) Prices	(4) Nat-ural fer-tility	(5) Sur-vival pros-pects	(6) Sub-jec-tive	(7) Mar-ket
	Demand, Cd			Supply, Cn		Regulation costs, RC	
1. Better public health and medical care				+	+		
2. Growth in formal education	−		−	+	+	−	−
3. Urbanization	−		−			−	−
4. New goods							
a. Consumer goods	−						
b. Fertility control						−	−
5. Family planning programs						−	−

Table 2.1 presents a summary view of the channels through which conscious family size limitation may be influenced by each of these aspects of modernization. In the table the specific modernization variables are listed on the left hand side, and the variables immediately relevant to deliberate fertility control—demand, supply, and regulation costs—at the top, as column headings. An entry in a cell indicates that the specified item on the left influences the variable at the top in the direction shown. For example, the negative sign in column 1 of row 4a indicates that, other things being equal, the introduction of new consumer goods during modernization tends to reduce the demand for children via its effect on the strength of preferences for children relative to goods. The effects shown in table 2.1 are illustrative; no attempt is made to be exhaustive. A brief sketch of the reasoning underlying the specific cell entries follows. (For a lengthier discussion, see Easterlin 1978; cf. also Nag 1983.)

Public health and medical care.—Improved public health and medical care impinges on the reproductive situation of the family by tending to increase potential supply in two principal ways. First, it may increase the natural fertility of women within marriage, though there are conflicting views on this (on the pro side, see Bourgeois-Pichat 1967a and Poston and Trent, 1984 (forthcoming); con, see Ronald Gray 1983). Second, even if natural fertility were unchanged, infants are more likely to survive to adulthood and potential supply would be correspondingly increased. These relationships are indicated in table 2.1 by the positive signs in columns 4 and 5 of row 1.

Better public health and medical care may raise per capita income, because a healthier, more energetic population is likely to be more productive (Malenbaum 1970). Increased per capita income, in turn, may influence demand and potential supply over and beyond the effects of better health just mentioned. However, to simplify the table, only the effects directly attributable to public health and medical care improvements are shown, not those that might indirectly be induced through the effect of better health on per capita income. The same treatment has been followed in table 2.1 with regard to the other aspects of modernization, each of which might affect per capita income as well as influence the adoption of deliberate control directly.

Education and mass media.—One of the most pervasive factors influencing fertility control behavior is the growth of formal education (Cochrane 1979, 1983). As shown in table 2.1 it operates on all three of the principal determinants—demand, potential supply, and regulation costs. The impact on potential supply is much like that in regard to the effect of public health and medical care improvements. Formal education improves health conditions by diffusing improved knowledge with regard to personal hygiene, food care, environmental dangers, and so on. It may also break down traditional beliefs and customs and thus undermine cultural practices, such as an intercourse taboo or prolonged lactation, which have had the latent function of limiting reproduction. In these ways it tends to enhance potential supply by raising natural fertility and/or increasing the survival prospects of babies; hence the positive signs in columns 4 and 5 of row 2.

Moreover, education tends to lower the costs of fertility regulation, as shown by the negative signs in columns 6 and 7. It may provide information not formerly available on various means of fertility control, reducing the expense in time and money previously required. It may also alter cultural norms adverse to the use of fertility control, and thus lower the subjective costs of fertility regulation, by challenging traditional beliefs and encouraging a problem-solving approach to life.

Finally, formal education tends to reduce the demand for children by shifting tastes in a manner unfavorable to children and decreasing the price of goods relative to children (see Lindert 1983). With regard to the relative price of children (row 2, col. 3), if better education improves the income-earning possibilities of women, then the alternative cost of the mother's time required in child-rearing is increased.

While some offset to this may be available, for example, through the help of other family members or domestic workers, there is probably some net positive effect on the cost of children and thus a tendency toward a reduction in the demand for children. In addition, compulsory education may increase the relative cost of children by reducing the possible contribution of child labor to family income.

Tastes for children, that is, the intensity of the desires for children relative to goods (row 2, col. 1), are affected negatively by education because children, and the life style associated with them, are essentially an "old" good, while education presents images of new life styles competitive with children. Also, education may lead to higher standards with regard to child care and rearing, creating greater emphasis on the "quality" of children at the expense of numbers. In these ways, education increases the subjective attractiveness of expenditures competitive with having more children, and thus tends to lower the demand for children.

Urbanization.—The process of modernization requires a redistribution of population from rural to urban areas that is accomplished in part by a vast increase in rural-urban migration. Urbanization reduces the demand for children by reducing tastes and lowering the price of goods relative to children (row 3, cols. 1 and 3). The mechanism of the effect via tastes is like that for education, by promoting antinatal life-styles. With regard to costs, the relative price of children of a given "quality" is usually higher in urban areas than in rural (Lindert 1980, 1983; Cochrane 1983). A variety of factors are responsible for this. The price of food is higher in urban areas than in rural. Also farm children take less time away from a mother's paid work and contribute more time toward family work than do urban children. In both cases, this would raise the relative cost of children in urban areas compared with rural. Thus, the effect of urbanization of the population is increasingly to place the population in an environment where goods become relatively less expensive than children, and, other things being equal, correspondingly more attractive.

In regard to potential supply, in the past urbanization probably had a significant negative influence, tending in itself to lower the survival prospects of children, because concentration in densely populated areas increased exposure to disease. However, this effect is less applicable under the more modern public health and medical conditions in urban areas in many of today's less developed nations than it was in the historical experience of the developed countries, and for this reason no entry appears in the table linking urbanization to potential supply.

Another mechanism through which urbanization might influence potential supply is by reducing lactation.

Finally, urbanization tends to reduce both the subjective and market costs of fertility regulation, via mechanisms much like those for formal education (row 3, cols. 6 and 7). In higher density urban situations, access to fertility control knowledge is likely to be greater, and market costs consequently reduced. Subjective costs too are likely to be less, because of the role of the urban environment in breaking down traditional attitudes, among them the reluctance to try new ways of doing things.

New goods.—Another facet of modernization is the continuing introduction of new goods (Rosovsky and Ohkawa 1961). In terms of the present framework, the introduction of new goods tends to lower the demand for children by shifting tastes in an adverse manner, as shown by the negative sign in row 4*a*, column 1. The enjoyment of new goods tends to require life-styles other than those centering on children, since new goods are typically substitutes for, rather than complementary with, children (Potter 1983; Mueller and Short 1983). At any given level of income, households would tend to shift expenditure toward new purposes and away from old goods, including in the latter, having and raising children.

Among the new goods associated with modernization are some specifically related to fertility control. Historical examples are the modern condom and improved methods of induced abortion; and more recently, the oral contraceptive pill and IUD. Such developments typically reduce the costs of fertility regulation by expanding alternatives. They may also lower the subjective drawbacks of fertility regulation by providing less objectionable options to the household. For example, an advantage claimed for both the pill and IUD compared with most other methods is that they separate the contraceptive act from that of intercourse. Allowance for the effects of new methods of fertility control is made in table 2.1 by the negative signs in columns 6 and 7 of row 4*b*.

Family planning programs.—Family planning programs chiefly affect regulation costs. The establishment of a network of family planning clinics (perhaps complemented by mobile units) offering services at below market prices reduces the time and money required to obtain information about methods, contraceptive supplies, and services such as insertion of an IUD or induced abortion. A family planning program may also reduce the subjective drawbacks associated with adoption of family size limitation techniques by providing social legitimation via publicity and demonstration for practices that might otherwise be viewed as alien to traditional culture. These influences on access to and attitudes toward family planning methods are shown in table 2.1 by the negative signs in columns 6 and 7 of row 5.

Some family planning programs explicitly try to promote the view that small families are desirable, and, to the extent such activities are successful, they lower the demand for children and thus increase motivation to limit fertility. At the extreme, measures to reduce demand might involve the imposition of explicit economic and social penalties for excessive fertility, as in China, although such policies are typically viewed as lying outside traditional family planning programs. Also, where family planning programs are integrated with maternal and child health care (MCH), they may have a positive impact on supply, by raising both natural fertility and child survival. Because the emphasis of most family planning programs is on attitudes toward and access to fertility control techniques, the effect shown in table 2.1 is confined to that via regulation costs.

Links from Supply, Demand, and Regulation Costs to Fertility Control and Fertility

The preceding section illustrates some specific ways that certain aspects of modernization affect the demand for children, potential supply, and costs of fertility regulation. This section extends the illustration by indicating how the latter three factors, in turn, may shape the trends in use of deliberate fertility control and childbearing as modernization progresses. As in the foregoing section, the discussion is hypothetical for lack of the requisite empirical studies.

Assume, to start with, that in a premodern society the typical couple cannot produce as many children as it wants, that is, that demand exceeds supply. This might be because of an agricultural environment that generates a high demand for children, or adverse mortality conditions and extended lactation making for a low supply, or a combination of the two. Under these circumstances a couple would have as many children as possible, that is, natural fertility would prevail.

Though the analysis of the preceding section is confined to only a few aspects of modernization, so far as it goes it suggests that modernization tends on balance to lower the demand for children, raise potential supply, and reduce regulation costs, and this is consistent with the general trend of other analyses. (See, for example, Lee and

Bulatao 1983; Bongaarts and Menken 1983; and Hermalin 1983.) The trends both in supply and demand tend to push a couple from an initial excess demand situation into one of excess supply, that is, in the absence of attempts deliberately to limit family size, the typical couple would have more children than are wanted. The prospect of unwanted children provides a motivation for family size limitation, say, via contraception; but such action is costly, both psychologically and economically, and the disadvantage of unwanted children must be weighed against these costs. Early in the modernization process the excess of supply over demand and, consequently, the motivation for fertility regulation are likely to be low, while regulation costs are likely to be high. As a result, the typical couple is likely to forego deliberate family size limitation and natural fertility will continue to prevail. Because modernization may be raising natural fertility, an increase in fertility may consequently be observed during this early phase of modernization (Nag 1980). However, as modernization progresses and the excess of supply over demand grows, the prospective number of unwanted children increases and generates a corresponding growth in the motivation to limit family size. Also, regulation costs and thus the obstacles to family size limitation are declining. At some point the balance between the motivation for regulation and costs of regulation tips in favor of the former, and actions deliberately to limit family size are taken. At this point the actual number of surviving children starts to fall below potential supply, though still exceeding demand. As modernization continues and motivation rises further and regulation costs fall still more—perhaps approximating a "perfect contraceptive society"—a point is eventually reached at which the actual number of surviving children corresponds to demand.

This analysis is represented schematically in figure 2.2. For simplicity of exposition, modernization is represented as a one-dimensional process, corresponding to a rightward movement along the horizontal axis. Supply and demand, measured in terms of surviving children, are shown on the vertical axis. Initially demand (Cd) exceeds supply (Cn), and the number of surviving children (C) corresponds to supply. As modernization occurs, an excess supply condition emerges (to the right of point m) generating a motivation for fertility control. Initially, this motivation is low and does not offset regulation costs sufficiently to result in deliberate family size limitation; hence the number of surviving children continues to correspond to supply. However, as modernization progresses, with motivation growing and regulation costs falling, at some point deliberate restriction sets in (to the right of

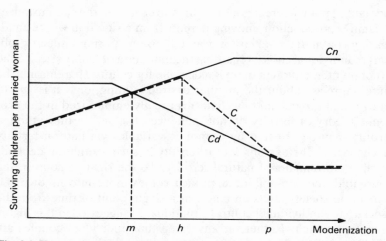

Fig. 2.2 Hypothetical Trends in Supply (*Cn*), Demand (*Cd*), and Number of Surviving Children (*C*) Associated with Modernization.

point *h*). With fertility control continuing to grow, the number of surviving children eventually falls to a level corresponding to demand (point *p*).

The precise nature of the trends in demand, supply, and regulation costs is, of course, a matter for empirical inquiries, such as those in the subsequent chapters. Moreover, as stated here, the transition starts from a premodern situation in which supply is less than demand and hence a motivation for regulating family size is absent. But there is nothing in the framework that requires this view. The premodern situation might be one in which motivation exists but the practice of fertility control is absent because regulation costs are very high (that is, the premodern position would be between points *m* and *h* in fig. 2.1). Clearly the true nature of the premodern situation is an empirical issue, and attention will be directed to this, especially in chapters 5 and 6.

Point *h* might be thought of as a dividing line or "threshold" between two modes of fertility regulation (Kirk 1971; United Nations Department of Economic and Social Affairs 1965). To the left of point *h*, fertility is "regulated" by a variety of social and biological mechanisms working through natural fertility, as in the Bourgeois-Pichat quotation of chapter 1. Fertility is not yet viewed by individual couples as involving a potential problem of unwanted children. The modernization process, which shifts the typical household to a position to the right of point h, creates a fundamental change in the circumstances of family reproduction, moving parents from a situation where child-bearing is a matter "taken for granted" to one posing difficult problems of individual choice regarding the limitation of family size. To the left of point h, although there is a demand for children parents may be quite imprecise about the number desired (stating, e.g., it is "up to God"), and the demand mechanisms usually emphasized in the economic theory of fertility do not influence observed fertility, though fertility may be affected by economic variables via natural fertility mechanisms. The explanation of fertility in such a situation depends on the determinants of natural fertility. To the right of point h, the household decision-making approach comes more into its own. Of course, no society shifts en masse at a single point of time from the "social" to "individual" control situations, as suggested in this highly simplified sketch. Rather, at any given time individual couples are distributed about the mean with regard both to motivation and regulation costs, and the modernization process pushes some couples across the threshold earlier than others; even under premodern conditions there may be some couples actually practicing deliberate family size limitation. Hence, at the societal level, there may be no "threshold" clearly identifiable in time. But if there are rapid and sizeable changes in supply, demand, or regulation costs that occur in common among many families (as an example see the reasoning of Retherford and Palmore 1983 and Retherford 1980), a societal threshold may be observable.

Theories of the Fertility Transition

The present approach may be further clarified by noting briefly how it relates to several well-known views on the causes of the transition from high to low fertility in modernizing countries. As will be seen, most theories usually focus on only one or two of the three key variables in the present framework.

Several theories, for example, either explicitly or implicitly stress influences working only through the demand for children. A statement in a recent article by economist Peter Lindert gives an excellent illustration (see also Schultz 1976):

> In all countries and all eras, fertility follows changes in the *demand* for children, driven by considerations of both economics and taste. Fertility fails to fall in the early phases of most countries' development, and falls thereafter, for a straightforward reason: the relative

costliness of extra children fails to rise until a fairly advanced stage in development. . . . It appears, therefore, that the fertility transition parallels the long-term pattern of child costs and benefits. (Lindert 1983, pp. 495–96, emphasis in original)

Anthropologist John C. Caldwell's "wealth flows" theory also stresses factors working wholly through the demand for children, though the underlying mechanisms shaping demand (intergenerational relationships) differ in important respects from Lindert's (Caldwell 1983).

In contrast, other analysts focus on supply. Consider, for example, Gosta Carlsson's (1966) well-known article on the historical experience of Sweden: "The Decline of Fertility: Innovation or Adjustment Process?" In terms of the present analysis, the adjustment process that Carlsson has in mind is the response that occurs when rising supply due to declining infant and child mortality pushes households across (or further to the right of) the fertility control threshold (point h in fig. 2.2). He contrasts this with an explanation of the fertility decline in terms of an "innovation," for example, in methods of fertility regulation that would, in the present terminology, reduce regulation costs. Carlsson argues that the Swedish evidence favors an interpretation of that country's fertility decline as an adjustment to increasing supply caused by lower infant and child mortality, rather than one arising from an innovation that lowers costs of regulation.

Still other scholars place primary stress on regulation costs. Knodel and van de Walle (1979) argue that the motivation for fertility control (an excess supply situation) already existed in many parts of Europe prior to the fertility transition: "There was latent motivation for reduced fertility among substantial portions of the population before fertility began to fall" and "births were frequently unwanted, especially among women" (pp. 226, 227). As regards the availability of or access to fertility control, they argue that "family limitation was not widely available or acceptable . . . [and] its use . . . [was] extremely limited because it was either unknown or objectionable" (p. 231). In consequence, they stress a decline in regulation costs as the key development behind the fertility transition: "We believe that what is understood by the 'cost of fertility regulation,' a term that covers a variety of factors including sheer familiarity with the concept and means of family limitation, is an extremely important component of an explanation of the secular fertility decline, as it occurred in Europe" (Knodel and van de Walle 1979, p. 239).

Others include some combination of demand, supply, and regulation costs. Ronald Freedman (1975), for example, places particular emphasis on two sets of social norms—those about family size and those about each of the "intermediate variables" of the Davis and Blake (1956) framework. The former would work through the demand for children. As regards the latter, norms regarding intermediate variables that are under voluntary control work through regulation costs; others relate to supply. As another example, Joseph Potter's (1983) and Geoffrey McNicoll's (1980) discussions of institutional influences primarily stress factors shaping the demand for children, either through costs or tastes, though in considering institutional influences on social values relating to "appropriate" fertility behavior, such as religious opposition to birth control, they touch also on influences on regulation costs.

By contrast with the foregoing views, while the present approach sees modernization as influencing fertility via supply, demand, and regulation costs, it does not adopt a particular theory of the relative importance of these variables, viewing this as a matter for empirical determination. To illustrate, suppose one wished to explain the fertility decline in a particular country in a particular period. Scholar A, following Caldwell's wealth flows theory, would concentrate on intergenerational relationships affecting the demand for children. Scholar B, impressed by Carlsson's analysis of Sweden, would look into changes in infant and child mortality underlying the supply of children. Scholar C, attracted by Knodel and van de Walle's emphasis on regulation costs, would inquire into factors affecting attitudes toward fertility control and access to family planning techniques. In contrast, the present theory says simply that the decline may be due to demand, supply, regulation costs, or some combination thereof. All three factors call for investigation, and not until the results of this analysis are in will one know on which factor or factors to focus in pursuing links to modernization. If, for example, it turned out that increasing supply had pushed parents into the adoption of deliberate family size limitation, then attention should center on the factors behind these supply changes. For this purpose, research on demand or regulation costs would be superfluous. Note, however, the qualification, "for this purpose"; in other places or other times, different factors may predominate—one might even conceive, for example, of a sequence in a particular country in which supply, demand, and regulation costs were each, in turn, dominant. Just as the present approach does not prejudge the relative importance of these factors, it does not hold that they have the same weights in all times and places. Nor does it claim that the same aspects of modernization are always dominant.

What is needed is empirical research, such as that to which we now turn, to help sort out the relative roles in the fertility revolution of supply, demand, and regulation costs, and their links to specific aspects of modernization. Such work will help assess the relative plausibility of theories such as the foregoing and to determine fruitful lines of further research.

II
Micro-Level Analysis
of Sri Lanka and Colombia

3
Model, Methodology, and Measurement

The next two chapters present a test of the supply-demand theory based on household data from the World Fertility Survey (WFS) for Sri Lanka and Colombia. The WFS data have the advantage of being comparable among countries, but, as is inevitably the case, the specific nature of the data constrains the type of test possible. The analysis in these chapters is a complete revision of that previously published in the authors' WFS report (Easterlin and Crimmins 1982) and reflects refinements of the model and estimation procedure. Although we obtain improved estimates of magnitude compared with our earlier WFS study, the general nature of the conclusions remains unchanged. Clearly, further refinements and exploration of alternatives are possible and desirable, but we feel that the analysis in its present form, and with the various tests for robustness presented subsequently, represents a reasonable micro level test of the theory.

This chapter presents first the formal model and then takes up, in order, issues of methodology, population coverage, and variable construction. Chapter 4 follows with the empirical results, including, in the appendix, tests for robustness. The analysis is guided throughout by a desire to use the same formulation in both countries in order to facilitate comparison.

The Model

For the analysis of household data, the theoretical approach of chapter 2 is conceptualized here in terms of a three-equation system. The first equation relates to the reproductive process, expressing a woman's total births over the reproductive career as a function of length of exposure to intercourse, fecundity, contraceptive use, etc.

To demographers, this equation corresponds to a proximate determinants analysis, the term we shall use to designate it subsequently; to economists, it is, in principle, a type of engineering production function. The second equation takes as its dependent variable one of the proximate determinants in the first equation, contraceptive use, and expresses it as a function of the demand for children, supply of children, and regulation costs; subsequently, this will be referred to as the "determinants of use" equation, or simply "use equation." This equation is the key one in testing the theory of chapter 2. The third equation (or, more appropriately, set of equations) expresses each of the independent variables in the first two equations as a function of modernization, cultural, and other factors. The first two equations correspond to the analysis of links from fertility and fertility control to demand, supply, and regulation costs, and the third, of links to modernization and other factors.

The proximate determinants equation is, specifically,

$$(1a) \qquad B = \alpha_0 + \sum_{i=1}^{i=7} \alpha_i X_i + \alpha_8 U + \epsilon$$

where the variables are

B = children ever born,
X_1 = duration of marriage in years,
X_2 = first birth interval in months,
X_3 = second birth interval in months,
X_4 = not secondarily sterile (NSS),
X_5 = months of breastfeeding in last closed interval,
X_6 = proportion of pregnancy wastage,
X_7 = proportion of child mortality,
U = use of contraception or induced abortion, measured in time since first use, and
ϵ = a stochastical disturbance.

This formulation is an attempt, subject to WFS data constraints, to implement at the household level Bongaarts's scheme for a proximate determinants analysis of national populations. In his pathbreaking work on this subject, Bongaarts identifies the following as "a complete set of intermediate fertility variables often encountered in reproductive models:"

1 proportions married among females
2 contraceptive use and effectiveness

3 prevalence of induced abortion
4 duration of postpartum infecundability
5 fecundability (or frequency of intercourse)
6 spontaneous intrauterine mortality
7 prevalence of permanent sterility

Each of these seven intermediate variables directly influences fertility, and together they determine the level of fertility. The first factor measures the extent to which women are exposed to regular intercourse (marriage is defined broadly to include consensual unions). The second and third factors measure the prevalence of deliberate marital fertility control, and the last four are the determinants of natural marital fertility. (Bongaarts 1982, p. 179)

Bongaarts's exposure variable, proportions married, is replaced in the present analysis by duration of marriage (including consensual unions), X_1, a measure more appropriate to analysis of individual households. His second and third variables are combined in the "use" variable, U. His fourth variable, duration of postpartum infecundability, is approximated here by three measures—second birth interval (X_3), duration of breastfeeding in the last closed interval (X_5), and the proportion of child mortality (X_7). Generally speaking, postpartum infecundability depends chiefly on breastfeeding behavior (Bongaarts 1983). Two indicators of this are used here, one relating to the first child (second birth interval) and one to the next to last child (breastfeeding in the last closed interval). The proportion of child mortality is included because child mortality may cut short breastfeeding and, hence, postpartum infecundability. Bongaarts's fifth variable, "fecundability (or frequency of intercourse)," is approximated by a couple's first birth interval. The reasoning is that in the absence of deliberate control, more fecund couples would, on the average, be expected to conceive sooner after marriage. The sixth variable, spontaneous intrauterine mortality, is measured here by the proportion of pregnancy wastage other than that due to induced abortion (X_6). Finally, the seventh variable, prevalence of permanent sterility, is reflected in an indicator of whether or not a wife is menopausal (X_4).

In addition to the variables enumerated above, several other possibilities were tried but found to be not statistically significant. These were age at marriage (both countries) and frequency of intercourse and length of postpartum abstinence (Colombia).

As regards the parameters of equation (1a), it is hypothesized that the cumulative fertility of a continuously married woman would be greater:

1. the less the use of deliberate fertility control by her or her husband ($\alpha_8 < 0$),
2. the longer her period of exposure, as measured by duration of marriage ($\alpha_1 > 0$),
3. the greater the couple's fecundability, taken to vary inversely with the length of the first birth interval ($\alpha_2 < 0$),
4. the shorter her period of secondary sterility ($\alpha_4 > 0$),
5. the lower her rate of fetal wastage (miscarriages, spontaneous abortions, and stillbirths), and hence physiological problems of reproduction ($\alpha_6 < 0$), and
6. the shorter the period of postpartum infecundability, reflected here in a shorter second birth interval, shorter duration of breastfeeding in the last closed interval, and a higher rate of child mortality ($\alpha_3 < 0$, $\alpha_5 < 0$, $\alpha_7 > 0$).

Following Bongaarts, we take the use variable, U, as a measure of deliberate fertility control, the X_2 through X_7 variables collectively as determinants of natural marital fertility and, with X_1 added, of natural total fertility (cf. also Bongaarts and Menken 1983). Thus, equation (1a) may be rewritten as

(1b) $B = N + \alpha_8 U + \epsilon$

where

$$N, \text{ natural total fertility, } = \alpha_0 + \sum_{i=1}^{i=7} \alpha_i X_i.$$

Differences among households in estimated natural fertility thus arise only from differences in the X_1 through X_7 variables.

As has been mentioned, the second equation expresses use of deliberate fertility control as a function of the motivation for control (the excess of supply over demand) and the costs of fertility control. Specifically, the second equation is

(2a) $U^* = \beta_0 + \delta(Cn - Cd) + \gamma RC + \mu,$

where

U = U^* if $U^* > 0$, otherwise 0,
Cn = potential supply of surviving children, = $(1 - X_7)N$,
Cd = demand for children,
RC = regulation costs, and
μ = a stochastical disturbance.

By hypothesis, the coefficient on motivation for fertility control, $Cn - Cd$, should be positive ($\delta > 0$) and that on regulation costs, RC, negative ($\gamma < 0$). Theoretically, Cn and Cd should have the same coefficient—the difference in behavior of two couples differing on $Cn - Cd$ by some given magnitude, and in other respects identical, should be unaffected by whether the source of the difference in motivation is Cn, Cd, or both. Subsequently this expectation is tested and confirmed.

The observable variables in equations (1a) and (2a) are the two dependent variables, children ever born, B, and fertility control, U, plus the independent variables relating to natural fertility, X_1, through X_7, the demand for children, Cd, and costs of regulation, RC. In the third equation each of these independent variables, in turn, becomes a dependent variable, a function of modernization, cultural, and other factors. Thus,

$$(3) \qquad W_j = \kappa_j + \pi_j Y_k + \rho_j Z_m + \eta_j$$

where

> W_j stands for each of the independent variables, X_1 through X_7, Cd, and RC,
> Y_k is a vector of modernization variables,
> Z_m is a vector of cultural and other variables, and
> η is a stochastic disturbance.

Conceptually, the specific Y and Z variables would be expected to differ among the various dependent variables; the determinants of breastfeeding, for example, are not the same as those of the demand for children. Also, even when a given determinant may be common to several dependent variables, it may exert its effect in different directions, for example, education may enhance child survival and reduce breastfeeding. Thus, the expected nature of the independent variables and their hypothesized effects differ depending on the dependent variable under consideration.

The formulation of the influences of modernization in equation (3) drastically compresses the analytical discussion of these influences in chapter 2, which was itself already a selective presentation. This compression is intentional, because the focus of the empirical analysis here is on the first two equations, those relating to links from demand, supply, and regulation costs to fertility control and fertility. There are two reasons for this emphasis. First, the operationalization of the theoretical framework was formulated in part with a view to using KAP-type survey data (surveys of knowledge of, attitudes toward, and the practice of fertility control). These surveys provide direct (though imperfect) measures of demand and regulation costs and a basis for estimating supply, and thus make it possible in the empirical analysis to de-link the second from the first part of the theoretical framework. Second, although the World Fertility Survey includes many of the typical questions of a KAP-type survey, it, like most KAP-type surveys, is thin on data relating to modernization, thus limiting empirical investigation of links with modernization; indeed, as we shall see, the variance explained by the standard WFS variables in total is typically quite low. In this respect the present emphasis is partly a matter of necessity.

In its emphasis on the first two equations, the present analysis bears similarities to recent work on the proximate determinants of fertility in that it provides a framework drawing on widely available data that offers the possibility of new insights into the determinants of fertility. In this case, the data are KAP-type data, and the insights relate to the relative roles in determining use of fertility control of the demand for children, supply of children, and regulation costs. At the same time, both approaches leave unsettled other important questions relating to the underlying socioeconomic processes at work. In an ideal world where theory was perfect and data unlimited, one would conduct a comprehensive and simultaneous analysis of the full system of equations. The compromise strategy adopted here is to exogenize the set of equations (3), subjecting the first two equations to intensive analysis, and to attempt only an exploratory analysis of the third set of equations. The remaining sections of this chapter are hence concerned exclusively with the intensive analysis of links from demand, supply, and regulation costs to fertility control and fertility.

Methodology

In this section we outline the econometric procedures employed and their rationale. These procedures were worked out in consultation with Professor David M. Grether, of the California Institute of Technology, and are based, in part, upon Maddala (1983, chap. 8).

The endogenous variables in equation (1a) and (2a) are children ever born (B) and deliberate use of fertility control (U); the exogenous variables are demand (Cd), regulation costs (RC), and the set of natural fertility determinants $(X_1$ through $X_7)$. A two-stage estimation procedure is used to obtain the parameters of (1a). First, the parameters of the following reduced-form equation, in which use of deliberate fertility control is expressed as a function only of the exogenous variables, are obtained by maximum likelihood (*ML*) estimation using a tobit procedure

(2b)
$$U = \lambda_0 + \sum_{i=1}^{i=7} \lambda_i X_i' - \delta Cd + \gamma RC + \mu.$$

The specific X_i' terms are shown in table 4A.2. The parameters of this equation are then used to obtain expected values of use from

(2c)
$$E(U_j) = V_j \cdot \Phi_j + \sigma \phi_j,$$

where

$$V_j = \lambda_0 + \sum_{i=1}^{i=7} \lambda_i X_{ij}' - \gamma Cd_j + \gamma RC_j \qquad j = 1 \ldots n$$

and Φ_j and ϕ_j are the distribution function and density function of the standard normal curve evaluated at V_j/σ (cf. Maddala 1983, eq. 8.4). These expected values of use are then used along with the observed values of X_1 through X_7 to estimate by ordinary least squares (OLS) the coefficients of equation (1a). Finally, each household's potential supply of children, Cn, is estimated as the product of its natural fertility, obtained as $\alpha_0 + \Sigma \alpha_i X_i$ for the household's X_1 through X_7, and its child survival rate. The household estimates of supply, Cn, are then used along with the household values of the demand for children, Cd, and regulation costs, RC, to obtain ML tobit estimates of the parameters of equation (2a).

In our exploratory WFS study, which emphasized simple techniques, we estimated (1a) directly by ordinary least squares. An objection to this is that the simultaneous nature of the model suggests that the use variable and the disturbance term in (1a) are likely to be correlated. As we shall see in the next chapter, there is evidence to this effect. Hence the present two-stage procedure was adopted in which an instrumental use variable was constructed from (2b) and (2c), and employed instead of the observed values of use to estimate (1a).

A second methodological innovation in the present study is that in estimating the use equations, (2a) and (2b), a tobit procedure was employed. This is because when use is measured in terms of years since first use, it can assume only zero or positive values, though there may be some households for whom conceptually a negative value would be meaningful. An example is a household that is unable to have as many children as it would like and, if the technology were available and cheap enough, would increase its fertility. Conceptually, such a household would, if it were possible, have negative "use" (family size "supplementation") rather than positive use (family size limitation). Because the use variable is truncated at zero, however, a number of households with varying degrees of low or negative motivation ($Cn - Cd$) are clustered at this value and an OLS regression line fitted to the data gives a biased estimate of the relationship of use to motivation. The solution to this problem is to employ tobit estimation (see Berk 1983, Maddala 1983). As will be explained below, it is also true that the sample population used for the analysis is truncated on the fertility variable, but a test indicates that the empirical effect of this is unimportant; hence, no tobit procedure was employed in this case.

To test the effect of these changes in methodology, we present in the appendix to chapter 4 comparisons of the parameters of (1a) and (2a) based on three estimation procedures. The procedures are (a) the current one, (b) OLS estimation of each equation (that used in our WFS paper), and (c) to test the effect of introducing tobit estimation, a variant of our current procedure in which (1a) is estimated by a standard two stage least squares procedure and (2a) by OLS. As will be seen, the signs and significance tests are almost always the same. However, the magnitudes of the coefficients are somewhat different depending on the technique used—especially the coefficients on the use variable in (1a) and motivation in (2a).

We considered using simultaneous estimation, but decided against it. The chief gain would be a further increase in efficiency of what are already, thanks to large sample sizes, quite precise estimates. The cost would be an even more cumbersome computational procedure. One might question also the appropriateness of such a refinement, given that we are estimating only part of a larger system.

With regard to functional form, linear relationships seemed appropriate in most cases. For example, with regard to the proximate determinants equation, one would expect, other things constant, that an additional year of exposure (marriage) would, other things constant, be expected to have the same impact in raising fertility whatever the initial duration of exposure (marriage). The importance of the ceteris paribus condition here should be underscored. For example, because of the possible early onset of menopause one might expect that the fertility impact of an additional year of exposure would be less the longer the duration of marriage. But in the present analysis, secondary sterility is controlled for, hence, one is, in effect, considering the impact of exposure under constant fecundity conditions.

Other relationships that we are considering might be expected to be nonlinear. Thus, there is evidence that the negative fertility impact of breastfeeding diminishes with duration of breastfeeding (Lesthaeghe and Page 1980). We experimented here and in several other cases with nonlinear functional forms, but generally found little change in the results. Given its computational simplicity, we chose, therefore, to use a fully linear model.

Finally, we preferred an arithmetic to logarithmic specification, because of an interest in absolute rather than relative magnitudes. For example, the coefficient on use provides a type of "births averted" measure, similar to those common in the family planning literature—measurement difficulties aside, the coefficient indicates the absolute reduction in fertility associated with one additional year of use.

The Sample

The study population is females near the end of their reproductive careers—those aged 35–44, who have been married only once (including consensual unions in Colombia), whose husbands are still living, and who have had at least two live births and no births prior to the start of their marriage or consensual union. The choice of those aged 35–44 is partly to control for age and partly to maximize the likelihood that variables such as first and second birth intervals would be observable. The restriction to continuous marriages minimizes conceptual and measurement problems associated with marital disruption. The theory does not encompass the causes of marital disruption, and accurate measurement of variables such as duration of exposure and use of fertility control becomes much more problematic for women with multiple marriages. The other exclusions arise from measurement problems alone. Women with premarital (or pre–consensual union) births are omitted because of lack of appropriate data on duration of exposure and first birth interval (X_1 and X_2). (In practice, this exclusion was only necessary for Colombia, because the proportion of women with premarital births in Sri Lanka was negligible.) For women with one child, there are, of course, no observations on second birth interval and breastfeeding in the last closed interval (X_3 and X_5); for childless women there are, additionally, no observations on first birth interval (X_2).

In Sri Lanka, the study population comprised about 73 percent of ever married females 35–44; in Colombia, 56 percent. The larger exclusion in Colombia reflects about equally the higher incidence there of marital disruption and premarital (or pre–consensual union) births, as the following tabulation makes clear:

	(1) Sri Lanka	(2)	(3) Colombia	(4)
	Number	Percent of line 1	Number	Percent of line 1
1 Ever married females, all parities	2237	100	942	100
2 Continuously married females, all parities	1789	80.0	651	69.1
3 Continuously married females, parities 2 and higher	1640	73.3	607	64.4
a. Excluding those with negative first birth interval	—	—	527	55.9

The actual number of cases reported in chapter 4 is somewhat lower than those in lines 3 and 3a, because of missing values on some variables.

Most of these exclusions tend to bias the sample toward women of higher fecundity. This is clearly so in regard to the exclusion of childless and one-parity women, because many of these women have sterility problems. Also, to the extent that marital stability in developing countries is a positive function of a woman's fecundity, a bias toward more fecund women arises from the omission of women with disrupted marriages. The one offsetting consideration is the exclusion of women in Colombia with one or more births prior to their union, since such women may be disproportionately fecund.

On theoretical grounds it is not clear how a bias toward more fecund women would affect the results, if at all. Based on the theory, one would expect that, other things constant, less fecund women would be less likely to contracept, because their potential supply (Cn) and, hence, motivation for fertility control $(Cn - Cd)$ would be lower than that of more fecund women. Hence, we are probably omitting a group with relatively low motivation and low use of fertility control. A partial test of the effect of this exclusion is reported below.

A second issue, raised by the exclusion of zero- and one-parity women, is that we are, in effect, truncating on one of the dependent variables, children ever born, with a consequent potential bias analogous to that described for the use variable. Reference to lines 2 and 3 of the tabulation just given shows that this exclusion accounts for only 8 percent or less of the population of continuously married women; in contrast, the zero observations on use of fertility control account for a third or more of all observations.

Because of these concerns about restriction of coverage to more fecund women, and truncation on the children ever born variable, we reran the analysis of chapter 4 including zero- and one-parity women, and, in Colombia, women with a birth prior to their union. We did not, however, attempt to include women with disrupted first marriages, because, as indicated, this would raise new theoretical as well as measurement problems. To include the omitted groups of women, we assumed values for the X_i variables for which no direct measure was available. The assumed values were, to the extent possible, in keeping with the conceptual nature of the variable under consideration. For example, to measure first birth interval for childless women, we assumed as a minimum value the woman's current duration of marriage plus nine months. As mentioned previously, first birth interval functions as a fecundity measure in the analysis and this assumption positions the relatively low fecundity childless women appropriately relative to others. The full analysis is reported in the appendix to chapter 4. As will be seen, the differences in results for the more comprehensive population are minor, suggesting that the problems discussed here are not a serious source of bias. We chose the restricted population as the focus of the presentation in chapter 4 because of reluctance to rely on what were inevitably arbitrary assumptions for the excluded groups of women.

Variable Construction and Interpretation

Eleven variables are involved in the proximate determinants and use equations, the two endogenous variables, children ever born (B) and use of fertility control (U), and nine exogenous variables, consisting of the set of natural fertility determinants, X_1 through X_7, plus demand (Cd) and regulation costs (RC). The specific construction of each variable is detailed in the appendix to this chapter. In this section we discuss those variables that raise special issues of interpretation, measurement, bias, or some combination thereof.

Fertility Control (U)

In this analysis, fertility control encompasses use of contraception, contraceptive sterilization, and induced abortion, whether for spacing or limiting numbers. Contraception includes both what WFS calls "efficient" methods (pill, IUD, diaphragm, condom, and injection) and "inefficient" methods (douche, abstinence, withdrawal, and rhythm). Breastfeeding was not included by WFS as a method of fertility control, presumably on the grounds that concern for fertility suppression is typically not important in determining breastfeeding practices. Although it is sometimes claimed that prolonged lactation is used as a contraceptive technique in parts of sub-Saharan Africa, recent studies tend to stress, not prolonged lactation itself, but a taboo on intercourse during lactation, motivated by concern for the health of mother or child (Caldwell and Caldwell 1977; Page and Lesthaeghe 1981; Mhloyi 1984). Knodel (1983, p. 71) cites fragmentary data for Malaysia and Taiwan on breastfeeding as a contraceptive technique, but these data relate to awareness, not use. His own subsequent and more probing inquiry in Thailand (Knodel, Havanon, and Pramualra-tana 1983) yielded negative results. Out of 23 "focus group" sessions believed to have tapped "major modal segments of the population," they found a clear consensus that breastfeeding would delay conception only among older women in one village. "Elsewhere . . . older women generally denied breastfeeding delayed pregnancy and often cited as evidence their own experience of becoming pregnant before they had weaned their child" (ibid., p. 19). For lack of good evidence to the contrary, we follow here the WFS practice of not treating breastfeeding as a contraceptive technique.

Respondents who reported no use of any of the fertility control methods above were assigned fertility control values of zero. For those who reported use, a rough estimate of years since first use was made by differencing current age and actual or estimated age at first use. Age at first use was specifically available for four methods—pill, IUD, condom, and sterilization. For the other methods, mother's parity after which use began was available. For these methods, age at first use was estimated as the mother's age at the birth of the child after which she first used fertility control plus, in Sri Lanka, two years, and in Colombia, one year. The one- and two-year adjustment factors were derived from the four contraceptive methods for which both age at first use and parity prior to first use were known. For the few women who used fertility control before any child was born, age at first use was assumed equal to age at marriage.

This measure of use clearly overestimates the duration of fertility control because it fails to take account of lapses from use. Our analysis suggests, however, that the measure does provide at least a rough measure of differences among users in the extent of use. For example, we tried as an alternative measure a simple ever used variable, in which all users were assigned values of one and nonusers zero, and found that the statistical explanation ($\bar{R}^2$) of children ever born in the proximate determinants equation was higher with years since first use than with ever used. This comparison is reported in the appendix to chapter 4. Another advantage of years since first use is that it enables us to analyze differences in fertility control behavior within the regulating population; this would not be possible with the ever used measure.

Other things constant, use of an efficient method might be expected to have a greater negative effect on fertility than use of an inefficient method, but a test failed to confirm this expectation. In the test a respondent's time since first use was multiplied by the efficiency of the method first used as reported by Bongaarts (1982). When used in the proximate determinants equation, this efficiency-adjusted measure was found to yield no improvement in the diagnostic statistics, and virtually no change in the coefficients.

First and Second Birth Interval (X_2, X_3)

For these variables, a minor problem arises in the case of those who used deliberate fertility control prior to their second birth. The proportions involved are small: in Sri Lanka, 10.8 percent, in Colombia, 13.8 percent. For these women, the second, and possibly, first birth interval variables are flawed as indicators of fecundability and postpartum infecundability. For lack of an alternative, the observed birth interval values for these users are replaced by the mean values for these intervals of those who did not regulate in that inverval.

Not Secondarily Sterile (X_4)

In the case of secondary sterility, the obvious choice for a measure was the response to a question on whether or not the respondent thought she could bear another child. However, according to this measure the average proportion of secondary sterility for continuously married women of all parities whose average age is about 39 years is unusually low, only 16 percent in Sri Lanka and 7 percent in Colombia. This compares with sterility estimates for women aged 40 by Henry and Vincent (reported in Pittenger 1973) of 32 to 33 percent.

After some experimentation, the following measure of secondary sterility was adopted: women were classified as secondarily sterile if (*a*) they reported a fecundity impairment, or (*b*) they were not currently regulating their fertility, had had no child in the last five years, and were not pregnant. This measure gave proportions of secondary sterility of 36 percent in Sri Lanka and 26 percent in Colombia for all women aged 35–44; for women with at least two children, the proportions are slightly less: 33 and 22 percent respectively. Those classified as secondarily sterile by this definition were assigned a value of zero on the variable; all others, a value of one.

Ideally, the measure of secondary sterility should be independent of knowledge about a woman's use or nonuse of fertility control, and in this respect this surrogate measure is flawed. A problem of potential bias arises from the fact that current use of fertility control (a zero/one variable) is one factor affecting the estimation of secondary sterility, which in turn enters into the estimate of Cn, one of the variables hypothesized to explain years since first use, the primary dependent variable in this analysis. Of course, current use is only one of four variables entering into the estimation of NSS, which, in turn, is one of seven entering into the estimation of Cn. Nor is current use identical with the dependent variable, years since first use. Some ever users (with positive values on years since first use) have zero values on current use, and current users differ among themselves in time since first use. One may doubt, too, that the NSS measure seriously misestimates secondary sterility, because it seems unlikely that a substantial number of current users would, in fact, be secondarily sterile. However, to make sure that our results would not be open to a charge of bias on this score, two tests were conducted. In one test, we used as the NSS measure simply self-reported fecundity, that is, whether or not the respondent thought she could have another child; thus NSS was defined entirely independently of use. In the second test, we employed the present NSS measure but confined the study population to current users only. For this population differences in use cannot be attributed to differences in NSS, because all current users have a value of one on NSS. Both tests, reported in full in the appendix to chapter 4, confirmed that our NSS measure does not account for our substantive results.

Proportion of Child Mortality (X_7)

This variable is the ratio for each woman of children who died to children ever born. Because the denominator includes a dependent variable, a criticism of possible bias might again be raised, in this case with regard to equation (1a). The empirical results reported in chapter 4 contradict this charge. If bias were a problem, one would expect a negative coefficient on X_7, but, in fact, we obtain a positive coefficient. Moreover, the effect on the results of including X_7 in the analysis is small. This is suggested by the fact that the coefficient on X_7 reported in chapter 4 is not significant in Sri Lanka and of only low significance in Colombia. As a further test, however, we reran the analysis dropping X_7 from equation (1a) and confirmed that the results reported in chapter 4 were virtually unchanged. This test is reported in the appendix to chapter 4.

Demand (Cd)

For this measure, the response to the following question was used: "If you could choose exactly the number of children to have in your whole life, how many would that be?" The value of the response to a question of this type is sometimes questioned. To the extent that skepticism arises from lack of simple correlation between observed fertility and desired family size, it is not relevant here. The present framework views desired family size as only one of a number of fertility determinants, and there is no necessity for desired size alone to be highly correlated with fertility. This point is illustrated in the analysis of chapter 5 (tables 5.4–5.6).

A more serious objection is that the response on number of children desired reflects the respondent's state ex post facto, that is after, not before, decisions regarding fertility and fertility control. Thus, actual family size may bias upward responses to desired family size, because children unwanted before the fact are reported as desired after the fact. There is, however, some evidence that the magnitude of the bias is not great enough to invalidate the usefulness of responses on desired size (Knodel and Prachuabmoh 1973). Especially to the point is a recent study of the change in family size preferences of two cohorts of Taiwanese women between 1965 and 1973 (Jejeebhoy 1981). No evidence was found of an increase in average desired size, despite the fact that these cohorts were at a stage in their reproductive career when most women were shifting from having fewer children than were desired to having more than desired. A subsequent Thailand study by

Kua Wongboonsin (1985) has yielded the same results. McClelland (1983, p. 319), after a comprehensive review of work on this topic, concludes that "it is not unreasonable to treat family size desires as measures of demand."

Potential Supply (Cn) and Natural Fertility (N)

A household's potential supply of children is not directly observable and is estimated here as the product of its natural fertility, N, and its child survival rate, s. We assume that the survival rate experienced by each household with regard to its actual fertility (B) applies also to its estimated natural fertility (N), that is, $s = 1 - X_7$. Because mortality tends to be slightly higher among higher parity children, this assumption results in a somewhat overstated rate of survival, but it seems doubtful that this is a serious quantitative problem.

Natural fertility is estimated for each household from equation (1a) as $\alpha_0 + \Sigma\alpha_i X_i$. It is unlikely, of course, that individual households form specific numerical estimates of their natural fertility as implied by this regression approach. Rather, the approach should be seen as an attempt at generalizing on how women pick up clues about their own natural fertility. Thus, the pace of early childbearing, prospective exposure (age at marriage, duration of marriage), fetal loss experience, evidence of fecundity problems such as irregular menstruation, and the like all probably contribute to a woman's assessment of her potential fertility, and, in turn, if the theory holds, to her motivation to deliberately control her fertility.

Because micro level estimates of natural fertility are unique to this study, it is not easy to evaluate these estimates. In work by the authors reported elsewhere several tests were run (Crimmins and Easterlin 1984). First, the mean of the micro level estimates obtained here for each country was compared with three macro level estimates—two following techniques based on Bongaarts (1978), and one based on Srinivasan and Jejeebhoy (1981)—and the present estimate was found to fall within the range of the macro estimates. (This work also showed that simple *OLS* estimation of equation (1) as in our WFS report yielded mean natural fertility estimates that were somewhat below the range of the macro level estimates.) As a second test, a comparison was made for each household between estimated natural fertility (N) and the actual number of children ever born (B), the presumption being that natural fertility should equal or exceed children ever born. In both countries this was found to be true in eight-tenths or more of the cases; in most of those where estimated natural fertility was less than actual fertility, the shortfall was usually only one child. A third test involved a micro/macro comparison of the contribution of various proximate determinants to differences in natural fertility, and was found to yield results roughly consistent with the literature. Based on these tests, we concluded that the micro level estimates of natural fertility in the present analysis are generally of reasonable magnitude.

Costs of Fertility Regulation (RC)

Conceptually, in measuring the costs of fertility regulation one would like data that reflect a household's subjective attitudes toward the use of fertility control, their information about methods of control, and the economic costs of obtaining additional knowledge about techniques of control and of purchasing supplies or services needed for control (cf. Hermalin 1983, pp. 19 ff.) Ideally such data would antedate the actual decision on fertility regulation, because one consequence of a decision to use control is likely to be a positive shift in users relative to nonusers with regard to both knowledge of methods and favorableness of attitudes. The measure(s) used must, of course, be available for all households in the study population; knowledge, say, of nonusers' attitudes toward fertility control is of little value unless one knows how they differ from the attitudes of users.

The measures available from WFS fall short of the ideal. The principal measure used here is the number of methods of fertility control known to the respondent and reported without special prompting, the idea being that greater knowledge makes use easier. We use unprompted reports of knowledge, rather than prompted, on the grounds that the former is a better index of the respondent's true knowledge. Several alternative measures are also explored, including the efficiency of the control methods known, and a measure relating to induced abortion: in Sri Lanka, whether or not abortion is known; in Colombia, the number of situations (out of a total of six) in which abortion is considered acceptable (the difference between the two countries in the abortion measure reflects data availability). In addition, the Colombia data include respondent reports on the accessibility of family planning services—the time required and distance to be traveled to obtain family planning services—though this information is reported by a considerably smaller number of respondents. All of these measures are defective on two counts: they fail to capture subjective feelings (except for the abortion measure in Colombia), which may be the most important part of costs of regulation, and they are ex post facto, that is, they reflect the respondent's state after, not before, the fertility control decision.

Although nothing can be done here about the omission of attitudes—such data were not collected by WFS—it is possible to some extent to test the proposition that the reporting of knowledge or accessibility may reflect use rather than vice versa. This problem relates primarily to the situation of regulators compared with nonregulators; within the regulating population there should be less differential bias arising from use. Hence, the analysis in chapter 4 is conducted not only for the total population, but also for the regulating population alone.

Appendix: Definition and Measurement of Variables

Variable	Country	WFS variable	Definition and measurement
Proximate determinants variables			
Children ever born (B)	Sri Lanka	V208	Number of children ever born.
	Colombia	Ditto	Same as Sri Lanka
Regulators, nonregulators	Sri Lanka	V634 S021	Reported ever using any method of contraception or induced abortion, 1 = yes (regulators); 0 = no (nonregulators).
	Colombia	V634 V204	Same as Sri Lanka.
Years since first use of fertility control (U)	Sri Lanka	S006 S009 S013 S017 S023 V009 V010 S007	If first method ever used was pill, IUD, condom, or sterilization, the age at first use is given by differencing year at first use of method and year of birth. If another method of fertility control was the first method ever used, age at first use is the mother's age at the birth of the child after which she first used family planning plus two years. If the woman used fertility control before any children were born, her age at first use is her age at marriage. The difference between current age and the age at first use is the years since first use of fertility control.
	Colombia	S215 S222 V009 S216 V010	If first method ever used was sterilization, age at sterilization is the age at first use. If another method was the first method used, the age of the mother at the birth of the

Variable	Country	WFS variable	Definition and measurement
		V204	child after which she first used plus one year is the age at first use. If the woman used fertility control before any children were born, her age at first use is her age at marriage. Years since first use is the difference between current age and the age at first use.
Duration of marriage (X_1)	Sri Lanka	V109	The difference between current age and age at first marriage.
	Colombia	Ditto	Same as Sri Lanka.
First birth interval (X_2)	Sri Lanka	V228	First birth interval in months. The mean first birth interval for regulators who did not regulate until after the first birth is substituted for the observed first birth interval of those who regulated before the first birth.
	Colombia	Ditto	Same as Sri Lanka.
Second birth interval (X_3)	Sri Lanka	B022 B012	The difference in months between the date of birth of the second child and the date of birth of the first child. The mean second birth interval for regulators who did not regulate until after the second birth is substituted for the observed second birth interval of those who regulated before the second birth.
	Colombia	Ditto	Same as Sri Lanka.
Not secondarily sterile (X_4)	Sri Lanka	V206 V402 V637 V225	Two-category variable: 1 = fecund; 0 = sterile. If currently pregnant, respondent is fecund. If respondent reports fertility impairment, respondent is sterile. If respondent is not a current user of contraception and reports no birth in the past five years, respondent is sterile.
	Colombia	Ditto	Same as Sri Lanka.
Length of breastfeeding (X_5)	Sri Lanka	V302	Number of months breastfed in last closed birth interval.
	Colombia	Ditto	Same as Sri Lanka.
Proportion of pregnancy wastage (X_6)	Sri Lanka	V201 V208	Number of wasted pregnancies divided by the sum of the number of wasted pregnancies plus the number of live births.

Variable	Country	WFS variable	Definition and measurement
	Colombia	V201 V204 V208	The difference between the number of wasted pregnancies and the number of induced abortions divided by the sum of the number of wasted pregnancies plus the number of live births minus the number of induced abortions.
Proportion of child mortality (X_7)	Sri Lanka	V213 V208	The difference between the number of children ever born and the number of currently living, divided by the number of children ever born.
	Colombia	Ditto	Same as Sri Lanka.

RC: *Costs of fertility regulation variables*

Variable	Country	WFS variable	Definition and measurement
Number of methods known	Sri Lanka	V601 V602 V603 V604 V605 V606 V607 V608 V609 V610 V611 V615	The number of methods of fertility control known to the respondent and reported without special prompting. Sum of "1" responses on variables listed.
	Colombia	Ditto	Same as Sri Lanka.
Efficiency of methods known	Sri Lanka	V616	Categorical variable: 1 = no method of contraception known; 2 = only inefficient method of contraception known; 3 = efficient method of contraception known.
	Colombia	Ditto	Same as Sri Lanka.
Knowledge of and approval of abortion	Sri Lanka	S021	Knowledge of abortion: 1 = heard of; 0 = never heard of.
	Colombia	S107	The number of situations (out of total of six) in which abortion is considered acceptable.
Distance to nearest family planning outlet	Sri Lanka	—	Not applicable.
	Colombia	S203	Number of kilometers to nearest family planning outlet.

Variable	Country	WFS variable	Definition and measurement
Travel time to nearest family planning outlet	Sri Lanka	—	Not applicable.
	Colombia	S205	Number of minutes' travel to nearest family planning outlet.
Motivation variables			
Supply, potential surviving children (*Cn*)	Sri Lanka	—	$(N \times s)$, where $N = \alpha_0 + \sum_{i=1}^{i=7} \alpha_i X_i$ in table 4.2, and s is $(1 - X_7)$.
	Colombia	—	Same as Sri Lanka.
Demand, number of children desired (*Cd*)	Sri Lanka	V511	Answer to question, "If you could choose exactly the number of children to have in your whole life, how many would that be?"
	Colombia	Ditto	Same as Sri Lanka.
Number of living children (*C*)	Sri Lanka	V213	Reported number of living children.
	Colombia	Ditto	Same as Sri Lanka.
Wants no more	Sri Lanka	V502	If respondent is fecund and wants no more children, wants no more = 1; if respondent is not fecund or wants more children = 0.
	Colombia	Ditto	Same as Sri Lanka.
Modernization variables			
Wife's education	Sri Lanka	S029	Number of single years of education.
	Colombia	V704	Same as Sri Lanka.
Residence	Sri Lanka	V702	Place of usual residence, 1 = rural; 0 = urban, estate.
	Colombia	Ditto	Place of usual residence, 1 = rural; 0 = urban.
Husband's occupation	Sri Lanka	V804	Dummy variable with categories: farmers (self-employed), agricultural workers (not self-employed), unskilled workers and laborers; omitted category includes white-collar workers (professional, clerical, sales), skilled craftsmen, and service workers (private household and other service and related workers).

Variable	Country	WFS variable	Definition and measurement
	Colombia	Ditto	Dummy variable with categories: farmers (self-employed), agricultural workers (not self-employed), service workers (not including private household workers); omitted category includes white-collar workers (professional, clerical, sales), skilled craftsmen, private household workers and unskilled laborers.
Wife's work status before marriage	Sri Lanka	V708	Dummy variable with categories: farm worker (either self-employed or not self-employed), nonfarm worker (worked in nonfarm occupation); omitted category is no work before marriage.
	Colombia	Ditto	Same as Sri Lanka.
Cultural variables			
Ethnicity	Sri Lanka	V707	Dummy variable with categories: Sri Lanka Tamil, Indian Tamil, Sri Lanka Moor; omitted category is Sinhalese plus others.
	Colombia	—	Not applicable.
Region	Sri Lanka	—	Not applicable.
	Colombia	V701	Dummy variable with categories: Atlantic, Oriental, Central, Bogotá; omitted category is Pacific.

4
Empirical Results and Tests

In the theory sketched in chapter 2, a new measure of motivation for fertility control is suggested, the excess of a household's potential supply of children over its demand. The main question of interest here is whether use of fertility control is positively associated with this measure of motivation, as the theory predicts, and if so, how this motivation measure performs compared with others used in the literature. Also of interest is the relative role of demand versus supply in shaping the motivation for fertility control, that is, whether high motivation is chiefly due to a high potential supply of children, a low demand for children, or both. The theory also predicts that use of control would vary inversely with regulation costs. Although some tentative impressions can be formed on this question, it cannot be fully resolved here because of inadequacies already mentioned in the measures of regulation costs available from WFS data. Finally, the analysis explores in preliminary fashion ways in which various aspects of modernization influence demand, supply, and regulation costs and through these, fertility control and fertility.

As already explained, the theoretical approach is conceptualized here in terms of a three-equation system (see chap. 3). The first equation is a proximate determinants equation, expressing a woman's total births over the reproductive career as a function of length of exposure to intercourse, fecundity, contraceptive use, and the like. This equation serves primarily two purposes: it provides the basis for estimating natural fertility, a major component of the potential supply of children, and it yields a specific quantitative estimate of the effect of fertility control on fertility. The second equation takes as its dependent variable one of the proximate determinants in the first equation, contraceptive use, and expresses it as a function of the demand for children, supply of children, and regulation costs. This equation is the key one in testing the theory of chapter 2. The third equation (or, more appropriately, set of equations) expresses each of the independent variables in the first two equations as a function of modernization and cultural factors. As explained in chapter 3, the first two equations—corresponding to the analysis of links from fertility and fertility control to demand, supply, and regulation costs—are the focus of the present analysis. The third equation, which relates to links to modernization and other factors, is treated only in an exploratory way in the last part of the chapter.

Links from Demand, Supply, and Regulation Costs to Fertility Control and Fertility

Proximate Determinants Analysis

As previously stated, the cumulative fertility of a continuously married woman (B) is hypothesized here to be greater:

1. the shorter the time since deliberate fertility control (U) was first used by her or her husband,
2. the longer her period of exposure, as measured by duration of marriage (or, in Colombia, consensual union), X_1,
3. the greater the couple's fecundability, taken to vary inversely with the length of the first birth interval, X_2,
4. the shorter her period of secondary sterility, X_4,
5. the lower her rate of fetal wastage (miscarriages, spontaneous abortions, and stillbirths), and hence physiological problems of reproduction, X_6, and
6. the shorter the period of postpartum infecundability, reflected here in a shorter second birth interval, X_3, shorter duration of breastfeeding in the last closed interval, X_5, and a higher rate of child mortality, X_7.

The means and standard deviations of these variables $(B, U, X_1$ through $X_7)$ and correlations among them are given in table 4.1. The simple correlation between the dependent variable, children ever born, and each of the independent variables has the same sign in both countries and the coefficients are often quite similar. The coefficients are low in magnitude, except that for duration of marriage. Moreover, the signs are in the hypothesized direction and significant, the only important exception being the correlations with breastfeeding, which, though not significant, have the wrong sign.

Table 4.1 Mean, Standard Deviation, and Correlation Matrix for Variables in Proximate Determinants Equation

Country and variable	Years since starting fertility control	Duration of marriage	First birth interval	Second birth interval	Not secondarily sterile	Months breastfeeding	Proportion of pregnancy wastage	Proportion of child mortality	Mean	Standard deviation
A. Sri Lanka (n = 1588)										
Children ever born	-.06*	.53*	-.13*	-.23*	.11*	.03	-.23*	.15*	5.68	2.54
Years since starting control		.07*	-.09*	-.13*	.26*	.03	.03	.00	4.28	5.78
Duration of marriage, years			.12*	.13*	-.28*	.22*	-.06*	.17*	19.83	5.65
First birth interval, months				.07*	-.01	.01	.18*	.06*	21.55	19.26
Second birth interval, months					-.12*	.13*	.05*	-.05*	29.20	19.50
Not secondarily sterile (= 1; others = 0)						.00	-.02	-.09*	.67	.47
Months breastfeeding in last closed interval							.00	-.12*	16.91	12.63
Proportion of pregnancy wastage								.04	.06	.12
Proportion of child mortality									.09	.15

B. Colombia (n = 507)

	(1)	(2)	(3)	(4)	(5)	(6)	(7)	(8)	(9)	Mean	SD
Children ever born		−.11*	.56*	−.05	−.17*	.11*	.05	−.11*	.23*	6.66	3.17
Years since starting control			.18*	−.09*	−.15*	.21*	−.20*	.05	−.08	7.26	6.58
Duration of marriage, years				.13*	.08	−.24*	.13*	−.01	.12*	19.41	5.15
First birth interval, months					.00	−.01	.04	−.01	.16*	16.77	13.57
Second birth interval, months						−.12*	.10*	.14*	−.09*	23.66	15.19
Not secondarily sterile (= 1; others = 0)							−.01	−.12*	−.11*	.78	.42
Months breastfeeding in last closed interval								−.09*	−.06	8.33	7.40
Proportion of pregnancy wastage									.06	.07	.12
Proportion of child mortality										.11	.17

*Significant at .05 level or better.

Among the independent variables, correlations are generally low; out of 56 correlations, the highest is only .28. Again, the signs and even magnitudes of the coefficients are often quite similar in the two countries. Although duration of breastfeeding is generally an important determinant of birth interval (Jain and Bongaarts 1981), the correlation coefficient here between breastfeeding and second birth interval (.13 and .10) gives little indication of redundancy. The breastfeeding variable refers, of course, to the last closed interval, and for only 10 percent or less of the study population in the two countries is the last birth interval the same as the second birth interval.

Turning to the results of the proximate determinants regression equation, one finds that in each country the expected directions of relationships hold (including, now, that for breastfeeding), and all but one of the coefficients are significant (table 4.2). The fitted equation accounts for 31 percent of the household variation in childbearing in Sri Lanka and 51 percent in Colombia. The standardized coefficients indicate a rough similarity between the two countries in the relative importance of the independent variables in accounting for household variations in children ever born: in order, duration of marriage, followed by secondary sterility and fertility control, then the two birth interval variables, and, finally, the breastfeeding and two mortality variables.

The metric coefficients are generally similar in the two countries, except for the two mortality variables. The impression of similarity is, however, somewhat misleading as regards duration of marriage. The coefficients of this variable, about .48 in Colombia compared with .33 in Sri Lanka, would imply a cumulative difference between the two countries of 3.0 births in a marriage of twenty years' duration.

As noted, one function of the proximate determinants equation is to provide a specific link between the use of fertility control and fertility. Setting aside considerations of correlation with the disturbance term the coefficient on the fertility control variable (U) indicates that in Sri Lanka, other things being equal, a household that started regulating its fertility, say, ten years ago would have 3.4 fewer births than a nonregulating household. For Colombia, the implied effect of the same degree of fertility control is fairly similar, 3.0 fewer births.

The other important function of the proximate determinants equation is to provide a basis for estimating natural fertility. This is obtained for each household in each country by substituting the household values on X_1 through X_7 in the equation in table 4.2, summing the results, and adding the constant term. In table 4.3 the mean levels of

Table 4.2 Proximate Determinants Equation: Second-stage Regression Results of Children Ever Born on Specified Variables

Country and statistic	Years since starting fertility control (U)	Duration of marriage (X₁)	First birth interval (X₂)	Second birth interval (X₃)	Not secondarily sterile (X₄)	Months breast-feeding (X₅)	Proportion of pregnancy wastage (X₆)	Proportion of child mortality (X₇)	Constant
A. Metric coefficient (standard error in parentheses)									
Sri Lanka	$-.3383^*$	$.3346^*$	$-.0324^*$	$-.0413^*$	2.6211^*	$-.0241^*$	-1.5966^*	.2842	1.0296
	(.0257)	(.0107)	(.0029)	(.0029)	(.1509)	(.0044)	(.4820)	(.3854)	
Colombia	$-.2989^*$	$.4809^*$	$-.0482^*$	$-.0494^*$	3.1637^*	$-.0597^*$	-1.0605	2.3383^*	$-.8217$
	(.0361)	(.0232)	(.0076)	(.0070)	(.2880)	(.0153)	(.8424)	(.6194)	
B. Standardized coefficient									
Sri Lanka	$-.3722$	.7319	$-.2496$	$-.3075$	.4810	$-.1203$	$-.0730$	.0159	
Colombia	$-.3616$	.7820	$-.2064$	$-.2368$	.4172	$-.1394$	$-.0403$	.1259	

C. Summary statistics	Number of cases	$\bar{R}^2$	F
Sri Lanka	1608	.31	93
Colombia	507	.51	69

*Significant at .05 level or better; adjusted standard errors are shown. First-stage regression results are given in table 4A.2.

Table 4.3 Mean and Standard Deviation of Estimated Natural Fertility and Children Ever Born, Nonregulating and Regulating Population

Country and statistic	Nonregulators		Regulators	
	Estimated natural fertility	Children ever born	Estimated natural fertility	Children ever born
A. Sri Lanka				
Mean	6.68	5.88	7.33	5.52
Standard deviation	2.11	2.54	2.11	2.53
Number of cases	712	712	875	875
B. Colombia				
Mean	8.18	7.18	8.90	6.43
Standard deviation	2.56	3.18	2.71	3.14
Number of cases	155	155	352	352

natural fertility thus obtained are compared with actual fertility for the regulating and nonregulating subpopulations separately. For nonregulators, those who never used fertility control, estimated natural fertility appears somewhat overstated, on the average, for it exceeds the mean number of children ever born, the true natural fertility of this population group. For regulators, the mean estimated natural fertility is, as would be expected, substantially above their actual fertility, reflecting their use of deliberate fertility control. Although the regulators' actual fertility is lower, on the average, than that of nonregulators, their estimated mean natural fertility is higher, with the same dispersion.

The finding that the estimated mean natural fertility of nonregulators exceeds their actual fertility (i.e., in terms of equation 1a of chapter 3, that $\bar{N} > \bar{N} + \varepsilon$ for those with zero use) implies that for this group the disturbance term in the proximate determinants equation is, on average, negative and, correspondingly, that for regulators is positive. This confirms the existence of a significant correlation in equation (1a) between the disturbance term and use, and thus the wisdom of the two-stage estimation procedure employed here.

It is possible to form a rough quantitative impression of the sources of the higher mean natural fertility of regulators than nonregulators by evaluating the specific contribution of each of the independent variables in the proximate determinants equation to the difference in estimated natural fertility. For each independent variable the excess of the regulator's mean value over that of the nonregulators, derived from table 4.4, is multiplied by the appropriate regression coefficient

Table 4.4 Mean and Standard Deviation of Variables in Proximate Determinants Equation, Nonregulating and Regulating Population

Variable and statistic	Sri Lanka		Colombia	
	Regulators	Non-regulators	Regulators	Non-regulators
A. Mean				
Children ever born	5.52	5.88	6.43	7.18
Years since starting control	7.75	0.00	10.46	0.00
Duration of marriage (years)	18.58	21.36	18.99	20.36
First birth interval (months)	20.82	22.45	16.02	18.48
Second birth interval (months)	26.27	32.79	22.14	27.10
Proportion not secondarily sterile	.88	.41	.87	.56
Months breastfeeding in last closed interval	16.04	17.98	7.46	10.32
Proportion of pregnancy wastage	.06	.05	.08	.07
Proportion of child mortality	.08	.10	.09	.16
B. Standard deviation				
Children ever born	2.53	2.54	3.14	3.18
Years since starting control	5.79	0.00	5.37	0.00
Duration of marriage (years)	5.78	5.09	5.24	4.82
First birth interval (months)	19.55	18.88	12.34	15.94
Second birth interval (months)	15.26	23.22	13.47	18.10
Proportion not secondarily sterile	.33	.49	.33	.50
Months breastfeeding in last closed interval	12.27	12.99	6.78	8.33
Proportion of pregnancy wastage	.12	.11	.12	.12
Proportion of child mortality	.13	.16	.15	.20
Number of cases	875	712	352	155

in table 4.2 This calculation indicates that the higher mean natural fertility of regulators is due chiefly to their lower incidence of secondary sterility, with a small contribution also made by their shorter birth intervals and duration of breastfeeding. The other proximate determinants, especially marriage duration, tend to lower the natural fertility of regulators compared with nonregulators, but their effect is outweighed by the variables raising the relative natural fertility of regulators.

Use of Fertility Control

In Sri Lanka the mean time since first use of fertility control is 4.3 years; for the regulating population alone, it is 7.8 years (tables 4.1 and 4.4). The corresponding figures for Colombia are 7.3 and 10.5 years. The theory hypothesizes that use of fertility control varies directly with the motivation for control, the excess of the supply of children over demand, and inversely with regulation costs. The three sections that follow examine the extent to which household differences in the use of control are related, first, to the motivation for control, second, to the costs of regulation, and finally, to the two determinants jointly. The analysis is conducted separately for the total population and the regulating population. Where appropriate, data for the nonregulating population are included for comparison.

Motivation.—Motivation, as measured by the excess of supply over demand ($Cn - Cd$), averages 1.7 children in Sri Lanka and 2.8 children in Columbia (table 4.5, panel A). For the regulating population alone the average is about 0.6 to 0.7 children greater than for the total population (panel B).

The greater the motivation, the greater is the expected use of fertility control. As an initial measure of the association between use of control and motivation, the correlation coefficients between the two variables are given below:

	Total population	Regulating population
Sri Lanka	.39	.34
Colombia	.42	.40

As expected, the relation is positive; moreover, the strength of the relation is similar for both the total and regulating populations and between the two countries. According to the usual tests, the correlations are highly significant. The percentage of the variance in years since first use of fertility control that is explained by the $Cn - Cd$ measure of motivation in a simple bivariate analysis is around 12 to 18 percent.

Table 4.5 Correlation Matrix for Years Since Starting Fertility Control and Specified Measures of Motivation for Total, Regulating, and Nonregulating Population

Country and variable[a]	Cn-Cd	Wants no more	C-Cd	Cn	Cd	C	Mean	Standard deviation
A. Total population								
Sri Lanka (n = 1588)								
Years since starting fertility control	.39*	.21*	.09*	.26*	−.15*	−.06*	4.28	5.78
Cn-Cd		.32*	.61*	.54*	−.51*	.01	1.74	2.17
Wants no more (= 1; others = 0)			.20*	.33*	.00	.15*	.74	.44
C-Cd				.39*	−.25*	.53*	.49	1.72
Cn					.45*	.69*	6.38	2.08
Cd						.69*	4.64	2.04
C							5.12	2.32
Colombia (n = 507)								
Years since starting fertility control	.42*	.19*	.12*	.37*	−.21*	−.09*	7.26	6.57
Cn-Cd		.40*	.81*	.60*	−.75*	.15*	2.79	3.88
Wants no more (= 1; others = 0)			.37*	.31*	−.24*	.19*	.80	.40
C-Cd				.43*	−.65*	.49*	.96	3.38
Cn					.08	.63*	7.61	2.57
Cd						.34*	4.82	3.12
C							5.79	2.72
B. Regulating population								
Sri Lanka (n = 875)								
Years since starting fertility control	.34*	.01	.04	.26*	−.10*	−.06	7.75	5.79
Cn-Cd		.27*	.59*	.55*	−.51*	.02	2.35	2.09
Wants no more (= 1; others = 0)			.21*	.33*	.05	.20*	.86	.35
C-Cd				.38*	−.24*	.56*	.65	1.74
Cn					.44*	.67*	6.73	2.01
Cd						.67*	4.38	1.94
C							5.03	2.28
Colombia (n = 352)								
Years since starting fertility control	.40*	.05	.06	.39*	−.17*	−.10*	10.47	5.37
Cn-Cd		.35*	.77*	.64*	−.71*	.19*	3.51	3.60
Wants no more (= 1; others = 0)			.29*	.27*	−.21*	.14*	.86	.35
C-Cd				.43*	−.60*	.58*	1.24	3.25
Cn					.09	.60*	7.98	2.53

Table 4.5 Continued

Country and variable[a]	Cn-Cd	Wants no more	C-Cd	Cn	Cd	C	Mean	Standard deviation
Cd						.31*	4.47	2.79
C							5.71	2.72
C. Nonregulating population								
Sri Lanka (n = 712)								
Years since starting fertility control	—	—	—	—	—	—	0.00	0.00
Cn-Cd	.24*	.65*	.48*	−.49*		.03	1.00	2.02
Wants no more (= 1; others = 0)		.16*	.27*	.04		.15*	.59	.49
C-Cd			.39*	−.24*		.50*	.29	1.64
Cn				.54*		.75*	5.95	2.10
Cd						.72*	4.95	2.11
C							5.24	2.36
Colombia (n = 155)								
Years since starting fertility control	—	—	—	—	—	—	0.00	0.00
Cn-Cd	.38*	.90*	.45*	−.80*		.13	1.16	4.01
Wants no more (= 1; others = 0)		.46*	.31*	−.21*		.33*	.66	.48
C-Cd			.40*	−.72*		.36*	.34	3.60
Cn				.19*		.79*	6.78	2.48
Cd						.39*	5.62	3.66
C							5.96	2.71

*Significant at .05 level or better.
[a]For definitions of motivation variables, see text discussion under Motivation; a dash (—) in this and subsequent tables denotes not applicable or not available.

How should one evaluate these results—do they favor or disfavor the theory of motivation advanced in chapter 2? One way of answering this is by comparing the statistical results with those obtained from alternative measures of motivation. The following are the possibilities explored here and their rationale (cf. Hermalin 1983, United Nations 1979):

1. "Wants no more children": Each respondent reported on whether she did or did not want more children, or whether she was undecided. It seems reasonable to suppose that those reporting that they want no more children were thereby motivated

to control their fertility. This is one of the most common measures of motivation used in the analysis of contraceptive use.

2. The difference between actual family size and desired size ($C - Cd$), sometimes termed "unwanted children": The hypothesis is that those who have more children than are desired are more likely to limit fertility. This measure differs from $Cn - Cd$ in that the household's actual rather than potential number of unwanted children is used (cf. Hermalin 1983).

3. Demand (Cd): The hypothesis is that those with a low demand for children are more likely to use control, that is, a negative association between use and demand is anticipated.

4. Actual family size (C): The hypothesis is that the larger the number of surviving children, the greater will be the use of fertility control. Essentially, this tests the view common in the literature that use is a function of parity (though parity is measured in terms of surviving children rather than children ever born, as seems more appropriate).

5. Supply (Cn): This is included for completeness, to compare with the results for C and Cd. The implicit hypothesis is that high potential supply fosters the use of fertility control.

How does the present measure of motivation ($Cn - Cd$) compare with these alternatives in explaining fertility control adoption? The results for the two countries are again remarkably consistent: the measure of motivation introduced in the present study, $Cn - Cd$, always performs best (see the top lines of the correlation matrices for each country in panels A and B of table 4.5). Among the other motivation measures, aside from actual family size (C), the direction of effect is always as expected and almost always significant. However, only one comes even close to $Cn - Cd$, and that is Cn, a component of the present measure. For the total population the subjective report on wanting no more children comes in a weak third; for the regulating population, this measure has no explanatory power at all. Contrary to expectation, the bivariate association of use with number of surviving children (C) is negative, though the coefficients are low and in one case, not significant.

In view of the questions noted in chapter 3 about the value of the measure of demand, desired family size, it is of interest to observe that, as expected, it uniformly bears a significant negative association with years since first use of control. However, when Cd is coupled with the measure of supply, Cn, to obtain the theoretically preferred measure of motivation, one obtains noticeably higher correlations with use than with Cn or Cd alone.

Sometimes use of fertility control is thought to depend on duration of marriage. It is pertinent to note, therefore, that none of the X_1 through X_7 variables, including duration of marriage, that enter into the estimation of Cn has as high a correlation in both countries with use of control as Cn itself, let alone $Cn - Cd$ (cf. table 4.1, line 2 of panels A and B, with table 4.5, panel A). In short, the present motivation measure does better in explaining use than its two components separately, Cn and Cd, better than the individual X_1 through X_7 components of Cn, and better than other measures of motivation often used in the literature.

The general similarity between the two countries in the rank ordering and magnitudes of the coefficients for both the total and regulating populations in table 4.5 is noteworthy, suggesting that in both countries the relationships within the regulating population and between the regulating and nonregulating populations are fairly consistent. One should not, however, assume that the pattern of correlations would be the same for countries differing widely from Sri Lanka and Colombia in the use of control. For example, in a country at a very early stage of adopting fertility control, one would expect that $C - Cd$ and $Cn - Cd$ would be quite similar in magnitude and have similar correlations with use of control.

Costs of regulation.—In general, years since first use of fertility control is expected to vary inversely with the costs of adopting control. As discussed in chapter 3, the cost measures actually available are deficient relative to the ideal, partly because there are no good attitudinal measures and partly because of ambiguity regarding the direction of the cause-effect relationship when the cost measures postdate the decision on use of control. Although we can do nothing here to correct for the lack of attitudinal data, we can, to some extent, deal with the cause-effect problem by analyzing separately the regulating population for whom this problem is much less serious.

Turning to the cost measures themselves, we find that in Sri Lanka, on the average, respondents spontaneously report knowing about two methods of fertility control; in Colombia, knowledge of methods is considerably greater, the mean number reported without prompting is over four (table 4.6). In both countries almost everyone, including nonregulators, spontaneously reports knowing at least one efficient method (note that the mean efficiency of methods known approaches the maximum of three in all panels of table 4.6). About 70 percent of respondents in Sri Lanka know of induced abortion, with little differ-

Table 4.6 Correlation Matrix for Years Since Starting Fertility Control and Specified Measures of Costs of Regulation, Total, Regulating, and Nonregulating Population

Country and variable	Number of methods known	Efficiency of methods known	Abortion	Closest family planning outlet — Distance	Closest family planning outlet — Travel time	Mean	Standard deviation
A. Total population							
Sri Lanka (n = 1588)							
Years since starting control	.24*	.18*	.10*	—	—	4.28	5.78
Number of methods known (unprompted)		.36*	.19*	—	—	2.08	1.55
Efficiency of methods known[a]			.20*	—	—	2.87	.49
Abortion (knows = 1; other = 0)				—	—	.70	.46
Colombia (n = 507[b])							
Years since starting control	.35*	.20*	.15*	−.14*	−.19*	7.26	6.58
Number of methods known (unprompted)		.32*	.20*	−.12*	−.21*	4.45	2.46
Efficiency of methods known[a]			.12*	−.16*	−.26*	2.94	.33
Abortion[c]				−.09	−.07	1.09	1.28
Family planning outlet: distance in km					.67*	3.83	8.44
Family planning outlet: time in minutes						27.30	50.06
B. Regulating Population							
Sri Lanka (n = 875)							
Years since starting control	−.05	−.06	.13*	—	—	7.75	5.79
Number of methods known (unprompted)		.17*	.20*	—	—	2.64	1.50
Efficiency of methods known[a]			.11*	—	—	2.99	.11
Abortion (knows = 1; other = 0)				—	—	.72	.45
Colombia (n = 352[d])							
Years since starting control	.15*	—	.08	−.12*	−.16*	10.46	5.37
Number of methods known (unprompted)			.07	−.11	−.14*	5.06	2.11

Table 4.6 Continued

Country and variable	Number of methods known	Efficiency of methods known	Abortion	Closest family planning outlet		Mean	Standard deviation
				Distance	Travel time		
Efficiency of methods known[a]		—	—	—	—	3.00	0.00
Abortion[c]				−.07	−.01	1.21	1.25
Family planning outlet: distance in km					.61*	3.45	8.12
Family planning outlet: time in minutes						23.72	38.33
C. Nonregulating population							
Sri Lanka (n = 712)							
Years since starting control	—	—	—	—	—	0.00	0.00
Number of methods known (unprompted)	.44*	.18*	—	—	—	1.38	1.31
Efficiency of methods known[a]		.26*	—	—	—	2.72	.69
Abortion (knows = 1; other = 0)			—	—	—	.68	.47
Colombia (n = 155[e])							
Years since starting control	—	—	—	—	—	0.00	0.00
Number of methods known (unprompted)	.38*	.32*	−.07	−.24		3.07	2.63
Efficiency of methods known[a]		.14	−.30*	−.33*		2.81	.58
Abortion[c]			−.10	−.18		.83	1.32
Family planning outlet: distance in km					.84*	5.57	9.69
Family planning outlet: time in minutes						44.09	84.56

*Significant at .05 level or better.
[a]Knows efficient methods = 3; only inefficient methods = 2; no methods = 1.
[b]Except family planning outlet variables, n = 302.
[c]Number of situations in which abortion is acceptable from zero to maximum of six.
[d]Except family planning outlet variables, n = 249.
[e]Except family outlet variables, n = 53.

ence between regulators and nonregulators. In Colombia, attitudes toward abortion are generally unfavorable; out of a maximum of six, the mean number of reasons cited as acceptable for induced abortion is about one, and regulators' attitudes are only slightly more favorable than those of nonregulators.

For these measures, one would expect a positive association with use of fertility control, because greater knowledge or more favorable attitudes would imply fewer obstacles to adoption, i.e., lower regulation costs. For the total population, this, indeed, proves to be the case—each of the measures shows a significant positive bivariate correlation with use (panel A, top line for each country). The measure that performs best is number of methods known, which accounts for 6 percent of the variance in Sri Lanka and 12 percent in Colombia. Efficiency of methods known comes in second, explaining 3 to 4 percent of the variance in both countries, while the induced abortion measures account for only 1 to 2 percent of the variance. Comparison of panels A and B of table 4.6 suggests, however, that the correlations between use of control and both number of methods known and efficiency of methods known are largely or wholly due to differences between users and nonusers; when the regulating population alone is considered, the correlations drop sharply, usually to insignificance. This result suggests that these measures of costs of regulation may, indeed, be showing the effects of use of control rather than vice versa. In Sri Lanka, the measure relating to induced abortion holds up better for the regulating population, but the level of correlation remains very low; in Colombia, the induced abortion measure also drops to insignificance for the regulating population.

The other measures of regulation costs relate to distance and time of travel to a family planning outlet, although these are available only for Colombia. In this case, the expected relation to use is negative— the greater the distance or time of travel to a family planning outlet, the lower the expected use of control. A problem with these measures is a sharp reduction in the number of cases. This is chiefly due to the disproportionate number of nonresponses among nonusers, suggesting that these measures too may reflect the use of control rather than vice versa. However, the correlations for the regulating population are not much below those for the total population, and for both groups they are negative, as expected, and significant (table 4.6, columns 4 and 5). As one would expect, time of travel appears to be a somewhat better indicator of accessibility than distance, although it accounts for only 2.6 to 3.6 percent of the variance in use.

Table 4.7 Correlation Coefficients between Specified Measures of Motivation and Regulation Costs, Total and Regulating Population

Country and measure of motivation	Measure of regulation costs	
	Number of methods known (unprompted)	Time to family planning outlet
A. Total population		
Sri Lanka (n = 1588)		
Cn-Cd	.16*	—
Wants no more	.14*	—
Colombia (n = 507[a])		
Cn-Cd	.15*	−.04
Wants no more	.02	.07
B. Regulating population		
Sri Lanka (n = 875)		
Cn-Cd	.05	—
Wants no more	−.02	—
Colombia (n = 352[b])		
Cn-Cd	.16*	−.08
Wants no more	−.07	.09

*Significant at .05 level or better.
[a]Column 2, n = 360.
[b]Column 2, n = 297.

Multivariate analysis.—Bivariate correlations show that the present measure of motivation, $Cn - Cd$, explains use of fertility control better than a number of alternatives; also, with regard to measures of regulation costs, that proximity to family planning outlets and number of methods known are best, although the former is only available for Colombia and the latter appears biased. The next question is how the motivation and regulation cost measures perform when put in competition with each other in a multivariate analysis. In considering this, we include also for comparison the alternative motivation measure, "wants no more," because it is one frequently used in the literature. As shown in table 4.7, the correlations between the independent variables—the measures of motivation and of regulation costs—are quite low.

As explained in chapter 3, the regression analysis allows for truncation of the dependent variable, that is, that use of fertility control cannot take on values less than zero. The results for the total popula-

Table 4.8 Tobit Regression of Years Since Starting Fertility Control on Specified Measures of Motivation and Regulation Costs, Total Population

		Metric coefficient (standard error in parentheses)						
		Motivation		Costs of regulation				
Regression number	Country	Cn-Cd	Wants no more	Number of methods known (unprompted)	Time to family planning outlet	Constant	Number of cases	χ^2
1	Sri Lanka	1.7534* (.1673)		1.9761* (.2278)		-6.8214	1608	382
1	Colombia	.9496* (.1426)		.9310* (.2186)		-1.2556	507	158
2	Sri Lanka		2.8714* (.4325)	1.0153* (.1135)		-4.5650	1608	268
2	Colombia		2.3277* (.6994)	.5338* (.1158)		-3.2078	507	104
3	Colombia	.8905* (.0889)			-.0187* (.0060)	4.6208	360	102
4	Colombia		4.5215* (1.0243)		-.0234* (.0068)	5.0417	360	28

*Significant at .05 level or better.

Table 4.9 Truncated Regression of Years Since Starting Fertility Control on Specified Measures of Motivation and Regulation Costs, Regulating Population

Regression number	Country	Metric coefficient (standard error in parentheses)				Constant	Number of cases	χ^2
		Motivation		Costs of regulation				
		$Cn\text{-}Cd$	Wants no more	Number of methods known (unprompted)	Time to family planning outlet			
1	Sri Lanka	1.3349* (.1570)		.3074 (.2048)		4.2260	898	88
1	Colombia	.6425* (.0872)		.2258 (.1500)		6.8413	352	52
2	Sri Lanka		.7925 (.9944)	.5481* (.2227)		7.4146	898	7
2	Colombia		1.3411 (1.0079)	.3843* (.1632)		7.1638	352	7
3	Colombia	.6762* (.0823)			-.0136* (.0069)	7.3391	297	62
4	Colombia		2.3906* (1.0778)		-.0198* (.0079)	8.8828	297	12

*Significant at .05 level or better.

tion are reported in table 4.8 and for the regulating population in table 4.9. (A comparison with OLS regression, not allowing for truncation, is given in the appendix to this chapter, table 4A.3.)

As regards the motivation for fertility control, the measure suggested by the present theory, $Cn - Cd$, consistently performs better than "wants no more" in every pairing of the two in tables 4.8 and 4.9. This is clear from comparisons of the χ^2 values and the t-statistic, the ratio of the metric coefficient to the standard error. Indeed, for the regulating population alone, "wants no more" is not significant in two of three regressions and barely so in the other. Regressions not published show that $Cn - Cd$ also performs better than the other motivation measures in table 4.5, the differences in performance looking much like those in the bivariate correlations. With regard to regulation costs, number of methods known performs well in the analysis for the total population but is not significant in that for the regulating population (see equation 1, tables 4.8 and 4.9), a result similar to that in the bivariate analysis. Time of travel to family planning outlets is consistently significant, though only marginally so for the regulating population. Finally, the t-statistic on $Cn - Cd$ is consistently higher than that on the regulation cost measures. Overall, then, motivation, as measured here by $Cn - Cd$, turns out to be the strongest and most consistent factor explaining use of fertility control. On the regulation cost side, accessibility to a family planning outlet, a measure available only for Colombia, is also consistently significant, though at a fairly low level.

As noted in chapter 3, in theory the coefficient on use of fertility control should be the same for Cn and Cd. To test this, the analysis was rerun with separate coefficients estimated for Cn and Cd. A χ^2 test confirmed that there was no significant difference between the coefficients on these variables.

From the analysis in this section one may draw some encouragement as to the value of the motivation measure used here. Given the roughness of the procedure for estimating a household's potential supply of children and questions about the meaningfulness of responses about the measure of demand, desired family size, one might justifiably have been skeptical of the prospective value of a motivation measure obtained from differencing the two. Yet, not only does such a measure vary with use of control in the expected way, but its explanatory power surpasses plausible alternative measures of motivation, stands up in the face of competition with measures of fertility regulation costs, and holds for both the total and regulating populations.

Proximate determinants of motivation and supply.—The evidence shows that use of fertility control varies directly with the motivation for control, as measured by the excess of supply over demand, $Cn - Cd$, and that the latter is a better measure of motivation than a number of alternatives. But what are the respective roles of supply and demand in household differences in motivation—does high motivation reflect high potential supply (Cn), low demand (Cd), or both? Similarly, since Cn is the product of natural fertility, N, and the child survival rate, s, to what extent are household differences in potential supply due to differences in natural fertility versus the child survival rate?

One indicator of the answers to these questions is provided by simple correlation analysis. Based on this, one finds that in both countries both supply and demand contribute to household differences in motivation. This can be seen from the following correlation coefficients, taken from table 4.5:

	Total population		Regulating population		Nonregulating population	
	$Cn - Cd$ with Cn	$Cn - Cd$ with Cd	$Cn - Cd$ with Cn	$Cn - Cd$ with Cd	$Cn - Cd$ with Cn	$Cn - Cd$ with Cd
Sri Lanka	.54	−.51	.55	−.51	.48	−.49
Colombia	.60	−.75	.64	−.71	.45	−.80

Though the correlations are generally somewhat higher in Colombia than Sri Lanka, the results are similar in both countries, namely, $Cn - Cd$ seems to be about equally correlated with Cn and Cd (the only serious exception is the nonregulating population in Colombia). This pattern of correlations reflects the general similarity in the standard deviations of Cn and Cd (compare table 4.5).

With regard to the proximate sources of household differences in supply, Cn, the role of natural fertility is more important, though differences in survival rates also play a part. The correlation coefficients in this case are:

	Total population		Regulating population		Nonregulating population	
	Cn with N	Cn with s	Cn with N	Cn with s	Cn with N	Cn with s
Sri Lanka	.86	.36	.87	.29	.85	.41
Colombia	.81	.39	.83	.32	.76	.44

Note that the results are about the same both between countries and between population groups.

One must be careful not to assume that results of this section, based on data for one point of time, necessarily apply to changes over time. For example, in a given country the distribution of households on the supply variable, Cn, might shift upward over time as a result of improvements in child survival common to all households, while the distribution of households on the demand variable, Cd, remained constant. The cross-section associations of motivation with Cn and Cd observed at any point in time might be of the kind found here, even though the increase in motivation over time was entirely due to a change in supply.

Births averted and unwanted fertility.—The approach used here lends itself not only to extending the analysis back into the sources of motivation, but also forward into the effects of the use of fertility control in terms of births averted and of nonuse in terms of unwanted fertility.

The excess of a household's actual number of living children over its desired family size is the implied number of unwanted children it has. In both countries both regulators and nonregulators have, on the average, more children than they want, but the excess is greater for regulators, despite their deliberate restriction of fertility (table 4.10, cols. 1 and 2). However, if one accepts the natural fertility estimates of

Table 4.10 Mean and Standard Deviation of Actual Unwanted Children (C-Cd) of Nonregulating Population, and of Actual Unwanted Children (C-Cd), Potential Unwanted Children (Cn-Cd), and "Children Averted" (Cn-C) of Regulating Population

Country and statistic	Non-regulating population	Regulating population		
	C-Cd	C-Cd	Cn-Cd	Cn-C
A. Sri Lanka				
Mean	.29	.65	2.35	1.70
Standard deviation	1.68	1.74	2.09	1.77
Number of cases	712	875	875	875
B. Colombia				
Mean	.34	1.24	3.51	2.27
Standard deviation	3.60	3.25	3.60	2.35
Number of cases	155	352	352	352

table 4.3, then if regulators, like nonregulators, had not controlled their fertility at all, the number of unwanted children they would have had—the excess of supply over demand, $Cn - Cd$—would have been considerably greater (col. 3). The success of their efforts at fertility control is given by the excess of potential supply over the actual number of surviving children—what one might think of as the number of "children averted" (col. 4). In both countries the number of children averted by regulators through fertility control is considerably greater than the number of unwanted children they actually ended up with; in effect, fertility control reduced the potential number of unwanted children by around 65 to 70 percent (col. 2 and 3).

The concept of "children averted" can be converted to the familiar "births averted" measure by dividing it by the child survival rate (the complement of the child mortality rate in table 4.4). When this is done, one finds that the mean number of births averted by regulators is about 1.8 in Sri Lanka and 2.5 in Colombia. (Alternatively, births averted can be derived from table 4.3 by differencing the regulators' values of estimated natural fertility and children ever born.)

Links from Modernization to Supply, Demand, and Regulation Costs

Ultimately, one wishes to identify the specific aspects of modernization influencing demand, supply, and regulation costs, and through these, fertility control and fertility. Because of the paucity of modernization data in the WFS survey, however, the analysis in this and the following section can only be exploratory. Unlike the preceding section, the purpose is not primarily to obtain substantive results, although some tentative impressions emerge. Rather it is to illustrate and further clarify the analytical links sketched in chapter 2, table 2.1. Because this is illustrative, the regulation cost measure used here is number of methods known, which, though less satisfying than proximity to family planning outlets, is available for both countries.

In this analysis, each of the independent variables of the preceding section, X_1 through X_7 (labeled here "determinants of Cn"), Cd, and RC, becomes a dependent variable, a function of modernization, cultural, and other variables (see chap. 3, eq. 3). For simplicity in the present analysis, we analyze a common set of independent variables, though in theory one would expect the independent variables to vary with the dependent variable under consideration.

In the initial phase of this analysis the independent variables consisted of virtually the entire set of standard background variables in the

WFS core questionnaire. Analytically, they fall into two groups: one is a set of "modernization variables," reflecting processes of socioeconomic development common to different countries (expanding education, urbanization, occupational shifts, and changing female work roles); the other is a set of "cultural variables," reflecting conditions peculiar to each country. In the first set the specific variables were education of both husband and wife, husband's occupation, wife's work status and occupation before and after marriage, and rural-urban residence, distinguishing within the urban category migrants from rural areas. In the second set, the variables were ethnicity and religion in Sri Lanka, and region and type of marital union (common law or other) in Colombia.

Regressions of each of the dependent variables on the independent variables (with the latter taken both individually and in various combinations) revealed that the following WFS core variables had little or no significant effect on any of the dependent variables: place of origin for urban residents, wife's work status and occupation after marriage, and type of marital union in Colombia. Also, some core variables were dominated by others: for example, husband's education was almost always dominated by wife's education, and, in Sri Lanka, religion by ethnicity. In addition, experimentation with various occupational groupings led to a fairly aggregative classification, emphasizing chiefly a farm-nonfarm division.

The results presented here are a distillation of the initial analysis and comprise the regression of each of the dependent variables on the remaining core variables. The modernization variables included are wife's education, rural-urban residence, occupational structure, and wife's work status before marriage; the cultural variables are ethnicity in Sri Lanka and region in Colombia. All of these variables are fully defined in the appendix to chapter 3. Their means, standard deviations, and correlations with each other and with each of the dependent variables are given in tables 4.11 and 4.12.

In both countries the dependent variables fall into two groups, based on the R^2 values and number of significant relationships in the regressions (tables 4.13 and 4.14). For one group, comprising four determinants of supply (first and second birth intervals, secondary sterility and pregnancy wastage), the proportion of variance explained by socioeconomic and cultural conditions is low or negligible (around 2 percent or less) and the independent variables are almost uniformly not significant. For these dependent variables it seems likely that differences among households are due primarily to genetic or phys-

Table 4.11 Mean, Standard Deviation, and Correlation Matrix for Variables in Modernization Analysis, Sri Lanka

Variable[a]	Wife's education	Rural residence	Farmer (husband)	Agricultural worker (husband)	Unskilled laborer (husband)	Farm work before marriage (wife)	Nonfarm work before marriage (wife)	Sri Lanka Tamil	Indian Tamil	Sri Lanka Moor	Mean	Standard deviation
A. Dependent variables												
Demand, Cd	−.30*	.15*	.15*	.03	.03	.05	−.21*	.04	−.02	−.11*	4.65	2.05
Number of methods, RC	.40*	−.18*	−.18*	−.14*	−.06*	−.14*	.28*	−.07*	−.06*	−.04	2.09	1.57
Duration of marriage	−.50*	.13*	.18*	.15*	.05	.16*	−.38*	.09*	.13*	.11*	19.81	5.63
Months breastfeeding	−.17*	.12*	.07*	.08*	.04	.10*	−.12*	−.04	.01	−.01	16.80	12.64
First birth interval	−.07*	.00	.02	.05	.04	.04	−.05	.05	.06*	.04	21.51	19.19
Second birth interval	−.05	−.04	−.03	.06*	.00	.05	−.03	.06*	.06*	−.02	29.49	20.54
Not secondarily sterile	.14*	−.01	.02	−.06*	−.04	−.04	.08*	−.08*	−.06*	−.04	.67	.47
Proportion of pregnancy wastage	.02	−.01	−.01	.03	−.03	.07*	.01	.00	.04	−.04	.06	.12
Proportion of child mortality	−.19*	.05	.02	.14*	.02	.15*	−.09*	.04	.16*	.02	.09	.15

B. Independent variables

Independent variables	(1)	(2)	(3)	(4)	(5)	(6)	(7)	(8)	(9)	Mean	SD
Wife's education	-.24	-.19*	-.27*	-.14*	-.37*	.33*	.05	-.26*	-.10*	4.36	3.51
Rural residence		.24*	.16*	-.06*	.22*	-.12*	-.11*	.11*	-.11*	.83	.38
Farmer (husband)			-.26*	-.21*	.15*	-.14*	-.04	-.11*	-.03	.29	.45
Agricultural worker (husband)				-.14*	.31*	-.15*	.02	.43*	-.04	.14	.35
Unskilled laborer (husband)					-.10*	-.02	.04	-.08*	.02	.10	.30
Farm work before marriage (wife)						-.22*	-.10*	.49*	-.11*	.20	.40
Nonfarm work before marriage (wife)							-.09*	-.12*	-.06*	.16	.37
Sri Lanka Tamil								-.11*	-.08*	.12	.32
Indian Tamil									-.07*	.08	.27
Sri Lanka Moor										.05	.21

*Significant at .05 level or better.

[a]Number of cases: for dependent variables, see table 4.13, line 12; for independent variables, 1637.

Table 4.12 Mean, Standard Deviation, and Correlation Matrix for Variables in Modernization Analysis, Colombia

Variable[a]	Wife's education	Rural residence	Farmer (husband)	Agricultural worker (husband)	Service worker (husband)	Farm work before marriage (wife)	Nonfarm work before marriage (wife)	Region Atlantic	Region Oriental	Region Central	Region Bogotá	Mean	Standard deviation
A. Dependent variables													
Demand, Cd	−.19*[b]	.16*	.08	.12*	−.12*	.18*	−.17*	.15*	.06	.02	−.16*	4.80	3.09
Number of methods, RC	.32*	−.34*	−.19*	−.19*	.12*	−.09*	.16*	.06	−.10*	−.02	.16*	4.45	2.46
Duration of marriage	−.22*	.15*	.09*	.12*	−.08	.06	−.24*	.12*	.00	−.03	−.05	19.37	5.18
Months breastfeeding	−.26*	.24*	.11*	.19*	−.08	.15*	−.09*	.19*	.08	−.16*	−.06	8.37	7.33
First birth interval	−.12*	.06	.02	.08	−.01	.08	−.01	.10*	−.01	−.10*	.00	16.71	13.67
Second birth interval	−.07	.04	.04	.03	−.02	.00	−.04	.05	.00	−.11*	.03	23.79	16.55
Not secondarily sterile	.10*	.02	−.03	.02	−.06	.01	.04	−.05	−.01	.06	.01	.78	.42
Proportion of pregnancy wastage	.12*	−.09*	−.05	−.05	.05	−.03	.01	−.01	−.06	.14*	−.03	.07	.12
Proportion of child mortality	−.28*	.20*	.04	.20*	−.09*	.17*	−.06	−.04	−.01	.06	−.08	.11	.17

B. Independent variables

Independent variables											Mean	SD
Wife's education	-.41*	-.18*	-.32*	.00	-.19*	.19*	-.10*	-.12*	.05	.24*	3.70	3.09
Rural residence		.38*	.54*	-.45*	.25*	-.30*	.07	.11*	.07	-.31*	.33	.47
Farmer (husband)			-.21*	-.31*	.11*	-.17*	.08	.04	.06	-.17*	.13	.33
Agricultural worker (husband)				-.46*	.13*	-.20*	.07	.02	.07	-.23*	.24	.43
Service worker (husband)					-.11*	.21*	-.09*	.01	-.08	.16*	.40	.49
Farm work before marriage (wife)						-.20*	-.04	-.04	.03	-.07	.05	.21
Nonfarm work before marriage (wife)							-.05	-.01	-.11*	.20*	.46	.50
Atlantic region								-.21*	-.29*	-.19*	.15	.36
Oriental region									-.33*	-.22*	.19	.39
Central region										-.30*	.32	.47
Bogotá region											.17	.37

*Significant at .05 level or better.
[a]Number of cases: for dependent variables, see table 4.14, line 13; for independent variables, 523.
[b]Husband's education.

Table 4.13 Regressions of Desired Family Size, Costs of Regulation, and Determinants of Supply on Modernization and Cultural Variables, Sri Lanka

Variable	Demand, C_d	Number of methods known, RC	Determinants of Supply, C_n						
			Duration of marriage	Months breastfeeding	First birth interval	Second birth interval	Not secondarily sterile	Proportion of pregnancy wastage	Proportion of child mortality
A. Metric coefficient (standard error in parentheses)									
Modernization variables									
1. Wife's education	−.1573*	.1414*	−.6471*	−.4015*	−.1678	−.2733	.0178*	.0011	−.0054*
	(.0166)	(.0121)	(.0403)	(.1070)	(.1670)	(.1886)	(.0040)	(.0010)	(.0012)
2. Rural residence	.5067*	−.2945*	.0566	1.8967*	−.8573	−2.9906	.0035	−.0057	−.0012
	(.1356)	(.0992)	(.3305)	(.8763)	(1.3720)	(1.5513)	(.0328)	(.0083)	(.0100)
3. Farmer (husband)	.2916*	−.4059*	1.3105*	1.0962	1.6478	−1.0282	.0361	−.0023	.0075
	(.1258)	(.0922)	(.3068)	(.8155)	(1.2744)	(1.4377)	(.0305)	(.0077)	(.0093)
4. Agricultural worker (husband)	−.0855	−.3684*	.6903	2.4660*	1.8755	1.4389	−.0005	.0024	.0261*
	(.1688)	(.1236)	(.4118)	(1.0920)	(1.7091)	(1.8795)	(.0409)	(.0103)	(.0125)
5. Unskilled laborer (husband)	−.0534	−.2189	.2030	2.0154	3.1448	−.5796	−.0196	−.0073	.0108
	(.1711)	(.1256)	(.4173)	(1.1064)	(1.7206)	(1.9056)	(.0415)	(.0104)	(.0127)

	(1)	(2)	(3)	(4)	(5)	(6)	(7)	(8)	(9)
6. Farm work before marriage (wife)	−.2359 (.1480)	.1467 (.1083)	−.8561* (.3609)	1.2926 (.9569)	.3002 (1.4900)	1.1515 (1.6764)	.0138 (.0359)	.0238* (.0090)	.0177 (.0110)
7. Nonfarm work before marriage (wife)	−.6109* (.1395)	.6132* (.1021)	−3.3547* (.3401)	−2.2533* (.9033)	−.6853 (1.4136)	−.8012 (1.6680)	.0322 (.0338)	.0031 (.0085)	−.0027 (.0103)
Cultural variables									
8. Sri Lanka Tamil	.3388* (.1505)	−.3585* (.1101)	1.6078* (.3670)	−1.5799 (.9730)	3.3836* (1.5122)	3.4816* (1.6612)	−.1304* (.0365)	−.0004 (.0092)	.0270* (.0111)
9. Indian Tamil	−.5436* (.2161)	.2264 (.1582)	.6571 (.5271)	−3.5442* (1.3974)	3.7701 (2.1795)	2.0130 (2.3855)	−.0716 (.0524)	.0018 (.0132)	.0456* (.0160)
10. Sri Lanka Moor	.7598* (.2310)	−.0594 (.1691)	1.5648* (.5634)	−1.2224 (1.4935)	4.1287 (2.3541)	−2.1542 (2.5511)	−.0623 (.0560)	−.0174 (.0141)	.0147 (.0171)
11. Constant	4.9646	1.8029	22.4815	16.7434	21.0724	32.5987	.5989	.0522	.0944
B. Summary statistics									
12. Number of cases	1634	1633	1637	1635	1593	1445	1637	1637	1637
13. $\bar{R}^2$	.133	.208	.314	.043	.009	.007	.027	.003	.053
14. $\bar{R}^2$, excluding lines 8–10	.122	.203	.304	.040	.005	.004	.020	.004	.047
15. F	26	44	76	8	2	2	5	1	10

*Significant at .05 level or better.

Table 4.14 Regressions of Desired Family Size, Costs of Regulation, and Determinants of Supply on Modernization and Cultural Variables, Colombia

Variable	Demand, Cd	Number of methods known, RC	Determinants of Supply, Cn						
			Duration of marriage	Months breast-feeding	First birth interval	Second birth interval	Not secondarily sterile	Proportion of pregnancy wastage	Proportion of child mortality
A. Metric coefficient (standard error in parentheses)									
Modernization variables									
1. Wife's education	-.1412*[a]	.1578*	-.2808*	-.3032*	-.3619	-.3096	.0146*	.0040	-.0129*
	(.0477)	(.0394)	(.0859)	(.1182)	(.2502)	(.3347)	(.0072)	(.0021)	(.0028)
2. Rural residence	-.1491	-.9730*	-.1864	1.0506	-.5043	-.7249	.0597	-.0101	.0087
	(.4240)	(.3257)	(.7112)	(.9860)	(1.9569)	(2.4342)	(.0597)	(.0172)	(.0231)
3. Farmer (husband)	-.3118	-.7238	.6804	2.2893	2.3645	3.7577	-.0683	-.0087	.0032
	(.5730)	(.4423)	(.9585)	(1.3300)	(2.6449)	(3.3862)	(.0804)	(.0231)	(.0312)
4. Agricultural worker (husband)	-.2823	-.2903	.6370	2.8430*	3.1947	2.6076	-.0117	-.0001	.0408
	(.5212)	(.3928)	(.8579)	(1.1829)	(2.3753)	(3.0743)	(.0720)	(.0207)	(.0279)
5. Service worker (husband)	-.6245	-.0810	-.1192	1.0746	1.5158	.8904	-.0535	.0112	-.0104
	(.3766)	(.2813)	(.6128)	(.8439)	(1.7060)	(2.2726)	(.0514)	(.0148)	(.0199)

	(1)	(2)	(3)	(4)	(5)	(6)	(7)	(8)	(9)
6. Farm work before marriage (wife)	2.2692* (.6494)	.3747 (.5003)	−.4103 (1.0974)	3.7379* (1.5354)	4.3406 (3.0068)	−1.6769 (3.7451)	.0430 (.0921)	.0019 (.0265)	.0854* (.0357)
7. Nonfarm work before marriage (wife)	−.5765* (.2786)	.2100 (.2158)	−2.1009* (.4696)	−.0605 (.6467)	.4689 (1.3058)	−1.2267 (1.6943)	.0444 (.0394)	−.0013 (.0113)	.0149 (.0153)
Cultural variables									
8. Atlantic	1.6967* (.4568)	1.0091* (.3515)	1.4038 (.7676)	3.5313* (1.0574)	2.4290 (2.1254)	−.6714 (2.7387)	−.0230 (.0644)	.0194 (.0185)	−.0296 (.0250)
9. Oriental	1.0029* (.4322)	.1733 (.3312)	.0896 (.7272)	1.4739 (1.0041)	−.7750 (2.0246)	−2.1856 (2.6052)	.0164 (.0610)	.0051 (.0176)	−.0143 (.0236)
10. Central	.6838 (.3877)	.4208 (.3004)	.0236 (.6551)	−1.2099 (.9035)	−2.3426 (1.8131)	−4.8207* (2.3704)	.0486 (.0550)	.0413* (.0158)	.0140 (.0213)
11. Bogotá	.0315 (.4610)	.5730 (.3603)	.9358 (.7759)	1.4132 (1.0713)	1.1716 (2.1771)	.6964 (2.8603)	.0063 (.0651)	−.0062 (.0187)	.0045 (.0252)
12. Constant	5.2716	3.8530	20.8596	6.9298	16.3704	26.0534	.6973	.0417	.1407
B. Summary statistics									
13. Number of cases	521	514	523	520	503	451	523	523	523
14. $\bar{R}^2$	.095	.156	.082	.133	.015	.000	.003	.019	.094
15. $\bar{R}^2$, excluding lines 8–11	.070	.146	.078	.090	.008	−.008	.007	.004	.094
16. F	6	10	5	8	2	1	1	2	6

*Significant at .05 level or better.
ªHusband's years of education substituted for wife's education.

iological factors rather than socioeconomic and cultural conditions. Of course, behavioral variables other than those included in the WFS core questionnaire might be significantly related to one or more of these dependent variables.

For the second group of dependent variables, some socioeconomic and cultural variables are significant and the proportion of total variance explained is higher, ranging from 4 to 31 percent. These variables include desired family size, number of fertility control methods known, duration of marriage, duration of breastfeeding and child mortality.

Considering all of the regressions together, one finds that the number of significant relationships is smaller in Colombia than Sri Lanka, perhaps in part because of the considerably smaller sample size there. It is noteworthy that among the modernization variables other than wife's farm work before marriage, all of the significant relationships in Colombia also hold in Sri Lanka, and in the same direction.

As a group, the modernization variables consistently dominate the cultural variables; when the latter are dropped out of the regressions, the proportion of variance explained declines only slightly. To the extent that one is interested in the implications of the analysis for changes over time, this result is encouraging, because the modernization variables change relatively rapidly compared with the cultural ones.

Among the modernization variables, wife's education is by far the most consistently significant. As mentioned, the initial phase of the analysis also showed that wife's education was consistently more important than husband's education (an exception was desired family size in Colombia). When husband's education was included together with wife's in the regression equations, the two usually eliminated each other from significance.

Next in importance among the modernization variables is wife's nonfarm work experience before marriage. For some of the relationships with this variable, however, the true cause-effect direction is open to question. For example, if a woman does not marry young, then the probability of her working before marriage and reducing her desired family size is increased. In this case, the causal variable is her marital situation, and work status and family size desires are effects.

A similar question regarding cause-effect directions might be raised about the negative relationship between wife's education and duration of marriage; if a woman marries later (i.e., has shorter marital duration), is she not likely to stay in school longer? In both countries, however, most women finish school long before they are married. In Sri Lanka women's schooling is completed, on the average, at 10.4 years of age; in Colombia at 9.7 years; these values compare with mean ages at marriage of 19.1 and 19.7 years. (Mean age at completion of school is estimated by adding 6.0 to the mean value for wife's years of education in tables 4.11 and 4.12.)

The other modernization variables that are occasionally significant are almost all linked to two processes that are partly associated: the shift from rural to urban residence and from agricultural to nonagricultural occupations. These variables include, specifically, rural residence, the occupational categories of farmer and agricultural worker, and wife's farm work before marriage, all of which would be expected to decline as modernization progresses.

Among the cultural variables, perhaps the most surprising result is found in Sri Lanka, where the ethnic group Sri Lanka Tamil turns out to be significantly different from the dominant Sinhalese group considerably more often than are Indian Tamils. Although both Sri Lanka and Indian Tamils are overwhelmingly Hindu, whereas the Sinhalese are chiefly Buddhist, the Sri Lanka Tamils share with the Sinhalese a Sri Lankan schooling experience, whereas the Indian Tamils do not.

In some of the individual relationships one finds results generally consistent with those commonly observed. Thus, in both countries family size desires are negatively associated with education and wife's nonfarm work before marriage (though for the latter variable some reservation has been noted about the causal relation). Knowledge of fertility control, as measured by number of methods known, is directly related to wife's education and inversely with rural residence. Also, marriages tend to be longer for wives with less education and no nonfarm work experience before marriage (although again the caution regarding the causal effect of the nonfarm work variable is applicable), and duration of breastfeeding is longer for women with less education or whose husbands are agricultural laborers. Finally, in both countries child mortality is higher among women with less education.

As has been mentioned, modernization would usually be accompanied by rising education, declines in rural residence and agricultural occupations, and an increase in women's nonfarm work before marriage. The present results for the dependent variables that are sensitive to modernization processes—family size desires, number of methods known, marriage duration, length of breastfeeding, and child mortality—indicate that the effects of these changes, when significant, are mutually reinforcing. In other words, each of the modernization processes works in the same direction on a given dependent variable. Moreover, the direction of effect (negative) is the same for all of the dependent variables except number of methods known.

Integrating the Component Parts: The Impact of Modernization on Fertility

This section aims to illustrate how the two preceding parts fit together analytically to link modernization to fertility. Because the prior analysis of links from modernization to supply, demand, and regulation costs was exploratory, the specific empirical results here are, at best, suggestive. Education is the aspect of modernization chosen for the illustration. The aim is to trace out the various channels—demand, supply, and regulation costs—through which ten years' difference in education between two groups of wives might be expected to affect their cumulative fertility by age 35–44, all other factors remaining constant.

The first step is to estimate the impact of the postulated difference in education on natural fertility. The previous section showed that education had significant effects on four determinants of supply: duration of marriage, secondary sterility, length of breastfeeding and child mortality (tables 4.13 and 4.14). Multiplying the ten years' difference in education by the regression coefficient of each of these proximate determinants on education, one obtains the implied difference in the variables due to education (table 4.15, col. 1–3). For example, in Sri Lanka the more educated group would be expected to have a marriage duration of about 6.5 years less than the less educated group; in Colombia, about 2.8 years less (lines 1 and 7).

The regression coefficient on each of these variables obtained in the proximate determinants analysis (table 4.2) enables one to convert the estimated difference in the proximate determinant to an estimated difference in natural fertility (table 4.15, col. 3–5). Thus, shorter marriage duration for the more educated group would reduce their natural fertility compared to the less educated group by about 2.2 births in Sri Lanka and by about 1.4 births in Colombia. In contrast, the effect of increased education on natural fertility within marriage is slightly positive. This is seen by comparing the effects of education on the proximate determinants other than duration of marriage: in both countries positive contributions from lower secondary sterility and shorter breastfeeding outweigh a negative contribution from reduced child mortality (table 4.15, col. 5, lines 2–5 and 8–11). Overall, how-

Table 4.15 Estimated Difference in Natural Fertility Due to Effect of Ten Years' Difference in Education on Specified Proximate Determinants

Country and variable	(1) Difference in years of education	(2) Regression coefficient of specified variable on education (tables 4.13 and 4.14)	(3) Difference in specified variable due to difference in education (col. 1 × col. 2)	(4) Regression coefficient of children ever born on specified variable (table 4.2)	(5) Difference in natural fertility due to effect of education on specified variable (col. 3 × col. 4)
A. Sri Lanka					
1. Duration of marriage, years	10	−.6471	−6.471	.3346	−2.165
2. Proportion not secondarily sterile	10	.0178	0.178	2.6211	.467
3. Months breastfeeding	10	−.4015	−4.015	−.0241	.097
4. Proportion of child mortality	10	−.0054	−0.054	.2842	−.015
5. Difference in natural marital fertility (sum of lines 2–4)	—	—	—	—	.549
6. Difference in total natural fertility (sum of lines 1–4)	—	—	—	—	−1.616
B. Colombia					
7. Duration of marriage, years	10	−.2808	−2.808	.4809	−1.350
8. Proportion not secondarily sterile	10	.0146	0.146	3.1637	.462
9. Months breastfeeding	10	−.3032	−3.032	−.0597	.181
10. Proportion of child mortality	10	−.0129	−0.129	2.3383	−.302
11. Difference in natural marital fertility (sum of lines 8–10)	—	—	—	—	.341
12. Difference in total natural fertility (sum of lines 7–10)	—	—	—	—	−1.009

Note: Differences in columns 1, 3, 5, are calculated as excess of more educated over less educated.

ever, the effect of increased education through shorter marital duration predominates, so that natural fertility among more educated
women is estimated to be lower than among less educated by about 1.6
births in Sri Lanka and 1.0 births in Colombia (lines 6 and 12).

The results of table 4.15 can be used to estimate the effect of
differences in education on supply, Cn. Analytically , the basis for the
estimate is given by:

$$\Delta Cn = \Delta s \cdot \bar{N} - \Delta N \cdot \bar{s} + \Delta s \cdot \Delta N,$$

where Δ refers to differences between the more and less educated
group on the indicated variable, $\bar{N}$ is mean natural fertility, and $\bar{s}$ is
the mean child survival rate.

In both countries the higher child survival rate of the more educated
group tends to raise their relative supply; the lower natural fertility
rate of the more educated, to lower their relative supply (table 4.16,
lines 3 and 6). The net effect of increased education in Sri Lanka is to
reduce relative supply, while in Colombia the net effect is negligible
(line 8).

The implications of the postulated difference in education for the
use of fertility control can next be estimated. For this purpose, in

Table 4.16 Estimated Difference in Supply, Cn, Due to Effect of Ten Years' Difference
in Education on Child Survival Rate and Natural Fertility

Variable	Sri Lanka	Colombia
1. Difference in proportion of children surviving (table 4.15, col. 3, sign reversed)	.054	.129
2. Mean natural fertility (table 4.3, weighted average)	7.04	8.68
3. Effect on supply of difference in survival rate (line 1 × line 2)	.38	1.12
4. Difference in natural fertility (table 4.15, lines 6 and 12)	−1.62	−1.01
5. Mean child survival rate (table 4.1, complement of proportion of child mortality)	.91	.89
6. Effect on supply of difference in natural fertility (line 4 × line 5)	−1.47	−.90
7. Effect on supply of interaction effect (line 1 × line 4)	−.09	−.13
8. Difference in supply, Cn, due to all sources (sum of lines 3, 6, and 7)	−1.18	.09

Note: Differences in lines 1, 4, 6, and 8 are calculated as excess of more educated over
less educated.

addition to the effect of education on supply, that on demand and costs of regulation is also needed. Based on an analysis similar to that for the natural fertility variables in table 4.15, one finds that in both countries ten years more schooling is accompanied by a reduction in demand of around 1.5 children, and an increase of about 1.5 in the number of fertility control methods known (table 4.17, col. 3, lines 2, 4, 7, and 9). The combined effect of the differences in supply and demand is a higher motivation for fertility control ($Cn - Cd$) among the more than less educated, though more so in Colombia than Sri Lanka (col. 3, lines 3 and 8). This estimated difference in motivation together with that in costs of regulation can be transformed into differences in years since first use of fertility control by means of the regression coefficients obtained in the fertility control equation (cols. 4 and 5). Overall, ten years more schooling is estimated to result in about 3.5 years' earlier use of fertility control in Sri Lanka and 2.9 years' in Colombia (col. 5, lines 5 and 10).

Previously, the results showed that education tends to reduce natural fertility, because the negative effect of education on marriage duration outweighs its positive effect on fertility within marriage. It is now possible to take account also of the effect of education on fertility arising from fertility control by using the regression coefficient of children ever born on use of control (table 4.2). When this is done, one finds that the higher use of fertility control among the more educated group of women reduces their fertility relative to the less educated by about 1.2 births in Sri Lanka and 0.9 births in Colombia (table 4.18, panel A). The overall effect on fertility of ten years' more education, including effects through both natural fertility and fertility control, turns out to be 2.8 fewer births in Sri Lanka and 1.9 fewer births in Colombia (table 4.18, line 9). In both countries, education reduces fertility both through marital fertility and duration of marriage, but its effect via the latter is greater (lines 7 and 8).

In sum, this illustrative analysis suggests that education tends to raise natural fertility within marriage, because positive effects through reduced secondary sterility and breastfeeding tend to outweigh a negative effect from reduced child mortality. The positive effect of education on natural marital fertility, however, is considerably outweighed by its negative impact on duration of marriage, yielding reduced natural fertility overall among the more educated. When, in addition, the effect of education on fertility control is considered, fertility is even further reduced. Education stimulates greater fertility control by increasing knowledge of methods of control and raising the

Table 4.17 Estimated Difference in Years Since First Use of Fertility Control Due to Effect of Ten Years' Difference in Education on Supply, Demand, and Costs of Regulation

Country and variable	(1) Difference in years of education	(2) Regression coefficient of specified variable on education (tables 4.13 and 4.14)	(3) Difference in specified variable due to difference in education	(4) Regression coefficient of fertility control on specified variable (table 4.8)	(5) Difference in years since first use of fertility control due to effect of education on specified variable (col. 3 × col. 4)
A. Sri Lanka					
1. Supply, *Cn* (table 4.16)	—	—	—	—	—
2. Demand, *Cd*	10	−.1573	−1.180	—	—
3. Motivation, *Cn-Cd* (line 1 minus line 2)	—	—	−1.573[a]	1.7534	.689
4. Costs of regulation, *RC*	10	.1414	.393	1.9761	2.794
5. Difference in duration of fertility control (sum of lines 3 and 4)	—	—	1.414[a]	—	3.483

B. Colombia

6. Supply, C_n (table 4.16)			.090	—	—
7. Demand, C_d	−.1412	10	−1.412[a]	—	—
8. Motivation, C_n-C_d (line 6 minus line 7)			1.502	.9426	1.416
9. Costs of regulation, RC	.1578	10	1.578[a]	.9310	1.469
10. Difference in duration of fertility control (sum of lines 8 and 9)			—	—	2.885

Note: Differences in columns 1, 3, and 5 are calculated as excess of more over less educated.

[a] Col. 1 × col. 2.

Table 4.18 Estimated Difference in Children Ever Born Due to Effect of Ten Years' Difference in Education on Fertility Control and Natural Fertility

Variable	Sri Lanka	Colombia
A. Difference in children ever born due to fertility control		
1. Difference in fertility control (table 4.17)	3.483	2.885
2. Regression coefficient of children ever born on fertility control (table 4.2)	− .338	− .299
3. Difference in children ever born due to fertility control (line 1 × line 2)	− 1.18	− .86
B. Difference in children ever born due to natural fertility (table 4.15)		
4. Due to natural marital fertility	.55	.34
5. Due to duration of marriage	− 2.16	− 1.35
6. Due to total natural fertility	− 1.62	− 1.01
C. Difference in children ever born due to all sources		
7. Due to marital fertility (sum of lines 3 and 4)	− .63	− .52
8. Due to duration of marriage (line 5)	− 2.16	− 1.35
9. Due to all sources (sum of lines 7 and 8)	− 2.79	− 1.87

Note: Differences in lines 1 and 3–9 are calculated as excess of more over less educated.

motivation for control. Increased motivation occurs because education reduces the demand for children.

The results of this analysis can be compared with those found by regressing children ever born directly on the set of independent variables in the modernization analysis of tables 4.13 and 4.14 above. When this is done, one obtains for the two countries almost identical significant regression coefficients on years of wife's education: − .2510 in Sri Lanka and − .2451 in Colombia. The effect of ten years' difference in education implied by the direct regression, about 2.5 fewer births among the more educated in each country, compares with values of 2.8 and 1.9 fewer births obtained by combining the equations of tables 4.2, 4.8, 4.13, and 4.14, as in this section.

The distinctive value of the present analysis is that it clarifies the number and variety of the mechanisms through which education operates. Thus, although direct regresion of fertility on education for Sri Lanka yields a coefficient almost identical with that for Colombia, the present analysis suggests that the relative importance of the mechanisms through which education works is somewhat different between the two countries. In a comparison of direct regressions of fertility on

education for a number of countries Cochrane (1983) finds wide variation in the regression coefficient, not only with regard to magnitude,
but even sign. The numerous links between fertility and education
brought out in tables 4.15–4.18 make clear why such variation might
occur.

Summary

Chapters 3 and 4 implement empirically and test the theoretical
view embodied in chapter 2's supply-demand framework of fertility
determination, using WFS data for two countries, Sri Lanka and
Colombia. The analysis focuses chiefly on a two-equation model that
links supply, demand, and regulation costs to fertility control and
fertility. The principal innovation is the measure of motivation for
fertility control. This is the algebraic excess of the supply of children
(derived from household level estimates of natural fertility and child
survival) over demand (respondents' desired family size). This measure performs best in explaining use of control in competition with a
number of alternatives. The implied interpretation is that those households that envisage unregulated fertility as leading to a family size
considerably in excess of that desired are under greater pressure to use
deliberate control. With regard to regulation costs, although the measures available from WFS data are somewhat flawed, proximity to
family planning outlets does show the expected effect on use of fertility
control, though this measure is available only for Colombia. This
effect, however, is considerably weaker than that shown by the present
measure of motivation.

The analysis also includes an exploratory inquiry into links from
modernization to demand, supply, and regulation costs. Although the
results for this part are highly tentative, they suggest that the independent variables fall into two groups differing in their sensitivity to
modernization factors. The variables more sensitive to modernization
influences are the demand for children, regulation costs, duration of
marriage, duration of breastfeeding, and child mortality; those that
seem largely independent are first and second birth intervals, secondary sterility, and pregnancy wastage.

Finally, the connections between the two parts of the analysis are
illustrated by tracing the various mechanisms through which one modernization variable, education, affects observed fertility. The variety
of links identified suggests why direct regressions of fertility on education yield highly different coefficients among countries.

Appendix: Tests for Varying Methods, Definitions of Use, Population Coverage, and Bias

Estimation Procedures

The first three columns of table 4A.1 present the proximate determinants equations obtained by the present method, two-stage least squares (2SLS), and ordinary least squares (OLS). (The first-stage equations for the two-stage procedures are given in table 4A.2.) In both countries and for all three methods the signs on the coefficients are the same and the coefficients that are significant are the same, with only minor exceptions regarding significance in the case of X_6 and X_7 in Sri Lanka. Also, the numerical magnitudes of the coefficients are usually quite similar, with the important exception of the coefficient on use of fertility control. In regard to the latter, in both countries OLS yields the lowest coefficient in absolute value; 2SLS, the highest; and the present procedure, a coefficient between the other two. Closer scrutiny shows that this is usually true also of the X_1 through X_5 coefficients, although the numerical differences are much smaller.

As explained in chapter 3, the present procedure is conceptually preferable, because of its treatment of the use variable as truncated in the first stage of the estimation procedure. Also, on empirical grounds, the present method appears superior. For example, the coefficient on the use variable yielded by 2SLS seems high in Sri Lanka—it seems implausible that a year's extra use would reduce fertility by more than a year's extra exposure (compare the coefficients on use and duration of marriage). On the other hand, the OLS coefficients on use seem low. This is suggested by comparison of macro level estimates of natural fertility based on the OLS equation with estimates independently obtained by methods used by Bongaarts and Srinivasan and Jejeebhoy (Crimmins and Easterlin 1984). In contrast, the present method yields estimates in the same range as those yielded by the methods of Bongaarts and Srinivasan and Jejeebhoy.

Because the natural fertility estimate varies depending on the estimation procedure used, the estimated supply of children and motivation for fertility control will vary by method of estimation. Panel A of table 4A.3 presents for comparison, therefore, the determinants of use equation for each of the three estimation procedures. In both countries and by all methods the coefficients on both motivation and number of methods known have the right sign and are statistically significant. Also, a replication of the analysis of tables 4.8 and 4.9 in the text, not shown here, shows that the conclusions reached in the text are the same for all three methods.

Considering the results for both the proximate determinants and use equations, therefore, we conclude that although varying methodologies have some effect on estimates of numerical magnitude, the basic conclusions reached in chapter 4 are the same irrespective of estimation procedure. We prefer the present method because of its conceptually superior treatment of the use variable as truncated.

Definition of Use

In this section, two definitions of use are compared—the present one, described in chapter 3, and a simple alternative where nonusers are assigned a value of zero and those who have ever used fertility control a value of one. The change in the nature of the use variable requires a change in method. We again employ a two-stage estimation procedure to obtain the proximate determinants equation. However, because the use variable is now a 0/1 variable, we employ a maximum likelihood logit estimation procedure in the first stage (see table 4A.2, col. 3). From the results of this equation, we construct an instrumental use variable and employ this in the OLS estimation of the proximate determinants equation. Also, in estimating the determinants of use equation, we again employ a logit procedure.

Comparison of columns 1 and 4 of table 4A.1 shows that the equations obtained with the two definitions are the same with regard to direction of effect of each variable and statistical significance. The magnitudes of the coefficient on the use variable are, as one would expect, quite different, but seem reasonably consistent. Thus, the Sri Lanka coefficient on ever used implies that users would have about 3.4 fewer children than nonusers, other things equal. By comparison, if the use coefficient in column 1 of $-.34$ is multiplied by the average time since users started controlling, 7.8 years (table 4.4), one obtains

Table 4A.1 Second-stage Regression Results for Children Ever Born (Proximate Determinants) Equation with Varying Definitions of Use and Estimation Procedure, Continuously Married Females Aged 35–44, Parities Two and Higher

Country and variable	Regression coefficient (standard error in parentheses)				Mean	Standard deviation
	U = Years since first use of fertility control			U = Ever used		
	Present method	2SLS	OLS	Logit/OLS		
A. Sri Lanka						
B, Children ever born	—	—	-.1101* (.0079)	-3.3752* (.3550)	5.73	2.56
U, Use of fertility control	-.3383* (.0257)	-.4379* (.0317)			4.32[a]	5.76[a]
X₁, Duration of marriage, years	.3346* (.0107)	.3826* (.0135)	.3196* (.0085)	.2771* (.0107)	19.94	5.61
X₂, First birth interval, months	-.0324* (.0029)	-.0384* (.0034)	-.0273* (.0023)	-.0264* (.0028)	21.94	19.76
X₃, Second birth interval, months	-.0413* (.0029)	-.0447* (.0034)	-.0358* (.0023)	-.0403* (.0030)	29.13	19.09
X₄, Not secondarily sterile (= 1; others = 0)	2.6211* (.1509)	3.0224* (.1810)	1.8093* (.0999)	3.0182* (.2094)	.67	.47
X₅, Months breastfeeding in last closed interval	-.0241* (.0044)	-.0214* (.0050)	-.0166* (.0035)	-.0261* (.0045)	17.07	12.79
X₆, Proportion of pregnancy wastage	-1.5966* (.4820)	-.9426 (.5642)	-2.6839* (.3770)	-2.0745* (.4859)	.06	.12
X₇, Proportion of child mortality	.2842 (.3854)	1.2091* (.4394)	1.1874* (.3057)	.7474 (.3857)	.09	.14
Constant	1.0296	.4225	.5890	2.3146		
Number of cases	1608	1608	1608	1608		
R̄²	.31	.40	.55	.30		

B. Colombia

					Mean	S.D.
B, Children ever born					6.66	3.17
U, Use of fertility control	−.2989* (.0361)	−.3435* (.0407)	−.1765* (.0157)	−3.9739* (.7317)	7.26[a]	6.57[a]
X₁, Duration of marriage, years	.4809* (.0232)	.5166* (.0261)	.4557* (.0200)	.3906* (.0236)	19.41	5.15
X₂, First birth interval, months	−.0482* (.0076)	−.0514* (.0079)	−.0452* (.0070)	−.0454* (.0088)	16.77	13.57
X₃, Second birth interval, months	−.0494* (.0070)	−.0540* (.0074)	−.0443* (.0064)	−.0476* (.0082)	23.68	15.19
X₄, Not secondarily sterile (= 1; others = 0)	3.1637* (.2880)	3.2901* (.3028)	2.6724* (.2413)	3.3201* (.3822)	.76	.42
X₅, Months breastfeeding in last closed interval	−.0597* (.0153)	−.0668* (.0161)	−.0373* (.0132)	−.0442* (.0176)	8.33	7.40
X₆, Proportion of pregnancy wastage	−1.0605 (.8924)	−.0301 (.8938)	−.7892 (.7923)	−.2492 (1.0126)	.07	.12
X₇, Proportion of child mortality	2.3383* (.6194)	2.3274* (.6421)	3.0125* (.5639)	1.9829* (.7663)	.11	.17
Constant	−.8217	−.9836	−1.1401	1.3021		
Number of cases	507	507	507	507		
R̄²	.51	.51	.57	.33		

*Significant at .05 level or better; adjusted standard errors are shown.
[a]For ever used, the mean and standard deviation for Sri Lanka are, respectively, .56 and .50; for Colombia, .69 and .46.

Table 4A.2 First-stage Regression Results for Children Ever Born (Proximate Determinants) Equation with Varying Definitions of Use and Estimation Procedure, Continuously Married Females Aged 35–44, Parities Two and Higher

Country and variable	Regression coefficient (standard error in parentheses)			Mean	Standard deviation
	U = Years since first use of fertility control		U = Ever used		
	Present method	2SLS	Logit/OLS		
A. Sri Lanka					
U, duration of use	—	—	—	4.32[a]	5.76[a]
$X_1 (1-X_7)$	.6140*	.4215*	.0378*	18.10	5.57
	(.0568)	(.0303)	(.0157)		
$X_2 (1-X_7)$	−.0788*	−.0493*	−.0107*	19.84	17.95
	(.0136)	(.0074)	(.0036)		
$X_3 (1-X_7)$	−.0950*	−.0431*	−.0194*	26.78	18.52
	(.0154)	(.0074)	(.0040)		
$X_4 (1-X_7)$	8.9762*	4.2945*	2.6788*	.62	.45
	(.5890)	(.3193)	(.1688)		
$X_5 (1-X_7)$	−.0337	−.0126	−.0185*	15.79	11.98
	(.0211)	(.0114)	(.0057)		
$X_6 (1-X_7)$	7.1535*	3.8977*	1.7803*	.05	.11
	(2.1625)	(1.2012)	(.6300)		
X_7	1.8567	7.7722*	.7494	.09	.14
	(3.7504)	(2.0253)	(.9561)		
X_7^2	11.2173	−.7857	−.5665	.03	.07
	(7.4650)	(3.8808)	(1.7519)		
Cd	−1.3880*	−.8028*	−.2159*	4.65	2.05
	(.1362)	(.0712)	(.0356)		
RC	1.6014*	.7712*	.5331*	2.06	1.53
	(.1649)	(.0898)	(.0495)		
Constant	−9.6821	−2.3289	−1.2372		
Number of cases	1608	1608	1608		
χ^2	514	—	665		
$\bar{R}^2$	—	.23	—		

Table 4A.2 Continued

| Country and variable | Regression coefficient (standard error in parentheses) | | | Mean | Standard deviation |
| | $U =$ Years since first use of fertility control | | $U =$ Ever used | | |
	Present method	2SLS	Logit/OLS		
B. Colombia					
U, duration of use	—	—	—	7.26[a]	6.57[a]
$X_1 (1\text{-}X_7)$	.5906*	.5194*	.0407	17.14	5.32
	(.0820)	(.0564)	(.0281)		
$X_2 (1\text{-}X_7)$	−.0917*	−.0699*	−.0213*	14.55	11.60
	(.0312)	(.0214)	(.0096)		
$X_3 (1\text{-}X_7)$	−.0924*	−.0640*	−.0220*	21.24	15.03
	(.0259)	(.0176)	(.0082)		
$X_4 (1\text{-}X_7)$	5.9417*	4.3583*	2.2187*	.75	.43
	(.9023)	(.6833)	(.3125)		
$X_5 (1\text{-}X_7)$	−.1954*	−.1305*	−.0380*	7.50	6.95
	(.0544)	(.0375)	(.0173)		
$X_6 (1\text{-}X_7)$	6.7471*	4.9065*	2.4818*	.01	.08
	(3.2422)	(2.3221)	(1.1662)		
X_7	.8839	7.2317*	−1.0723	.11	.17
	(4.6963)	(3.3598)	(1.5069)		
X_7^2	9.8653	2.0036	1.4292	.04	.11
	(7.5670)	(5.0266)	(2.2201)		
Cd	−.5630*	−.4286*	−.0827*	4.82	3.12
	(.1211)	(.0806)	(.0357)		
RC	1.2615	.8264*	.3607*	4.45	2.46
	(1.5259)	(.1034)	(.0528)		
Constant	−8.1541	−4.1278	−1.3595		
Number of cases	507	507	507		
χ^2	202	—	162		
$\bar{R}^2$	—	.31	—		

*Significant at .05 level or better.
[a]For ever used, the mean and standard deviation for Sri Lanka are, respectively, .56 and .50; for Colombia, .69 and .46.

Table 4A.3 Regression Results for Determinants of Use Equation with Varying Definitions of Use and Estimation Procedure, Continuously Married Females Aged 35–44, Parities Two and Higher

Country, and variable	Regression coefficient (standard error in parentheses)				Mean (standard deviation in parentheses)			
	U = Years since first use of fertility control			U = Ever used	U = Years since first use of fertility control			U = Ever used
	Present method	2SLS	OLS	Logit/OLS	Present method	2SLS	OLS	Logit/OLS
A. Sri Lanka								
Use of fertility control	—	—	—	—	4.32 (5.76)	4.32 (5.76)	4.32 (5.76)	.56 (.50)
Cn-Cd	1.7534* (.1673)	.9296* (.0560)	.9526* (.0648)	.3302* (.0289)	1.78 (2.20)	2.25 (2.32)	.96 (2.03)	2.26 (2.21)
Number of methods known	1.9761* (.2278)	.7371* (.0849)	.7935* (.0860)	.5970* (.0448)	2.06 (1.53)	2.06 (1.53)	2.06 (1.53)	2.06 (1.53)
Constant	−6.8214	.7016	1.7688	−1.6545				
Number of cases	1608	1608	1608	1608				
$\bar{R}^2$	—	.19	.17	—				
χ^2	382	—	—	430				

B. Colombia

Use of fertility control	—	—	—	—					
Cn-Cd	.9496* (.1426)	.6274* (.0640)	.6302* (.0689)	.1512* (.0289)	7.26 (6.57)	7.26 (6.57)	7.26 (6.57)	7.26 (6.57)	.69 (.46)
Number of methods known	.9310* (.2186)	.7786* (.1036)	.7974* (.1045)	.3446* (.0478)	2.81 (3.91)	3.21 (3.98)	3.21 (3.73)	2.14 (3.73)	3.46 (3.87)
Constant	-1.2556	1.7864	2.3681	-1.0702	4.45 (2.46)	4.45 (2.46)	4.45 (2.46)	4.45 (2.46)	4.45 (2.46)
Number of cases	507	507	507	507					
$\bar{R}^2$	—	.26	.25	—					
χ^2	158	—	—	105					

*Significant at .05 level or better.

an average reduction in fertility of 2.7 children. (For Colombia, the corresponding figures are 3.9 and 3.2 fewer children.) In Sri Lanka, the present measure of use yields an $\bar{R}^2$ higher than that for ever used, but only slightly so, .31 compared with .30; in Colombia, however, the present measure yields an $\bar{R}^2$ of .51 compared with .33. With regard to the determinants of use equation (table 4A.3), the signs and significance of coefficients are again the same. Thus, while the conclusions are largely unaffected by the definition of use chosen, the present measure of years since first use is, to judge from the $\bar{R}^2$ in the proximate determinants equation, somewhat more sensitive in picking up variations in fertility control among households. Also, years since first use enables us to analyze variations in fertility control within the regulating population, whereas all regulators have a value of one on ever used.

Population Coverage

The problem here is that there are no observations on several of the independent variables for zero and one parity women or for those with premarital births (the problem of premarital births is of negligible numerical importance in Sri Lanka); hence the analysis of chapter 4 is done for the population excluding these women. The excluded population amounted to about 10 percent of continuously married women in Sri Lanka and 20 percent in Colombia (see text, chap. 3).

To test whether the results would be much different for the more inclusive group of women, we reran the analysis including these women, making assumptions about the unobserved values which we felt were in keeping with the conceptual nature of the variable. Thus, for one parity women, a minimum estimate of second birth interval was made equal to months elapsed since first birth plus nine. Analogously, the first birth interval of zero parity women was assumed equal to duration of marriage plus nine; the second birth interval for these women was set equal to the mean interval of the observed values for other women, excluding those of women who regulated prior to their second birth. For one parity women, duration of breastfeeding in the last closed interval was assumed equal to that in the open interval, unless the woman was still breastfeeding. For the latter women and zero parity women, the observed mean length of breastfeeding in the last closed interval for other women was used. For women with premarital or preconsensual union births, first birth interval was assumed to be nine months, and duration of exposure was set equal to the period since first birth plus nine months.

The analysis for the larger population was run using three different estimation procedures—the present one, 2SLS, and OLS—and also for the alternative measure of fertility control, ever used. Table 4A.4 presents the estimates for the proximate determinants equation (first stage estimates are in table 4A.5) and table 4A.6, the determinants of use equation. Comparison with the corresponding tables (4A.1–4A.3) for the smaller population shows that the results are very similar. This conclusion holds irrespective of estimation procedure or definition of use. It seems unlikely, therefore, that the omission of these women from the text analysis in chapter 4 seriously affects the results.

Bias

The text of chapter 3 pointed out a possible problem in that one of the variables (NSS) entering into the estimation of a right-hand variable (Cn) in the use equation is partly constructed from data on current use of fertility control. Two tests were run to see whether our results were affected by this. First, we redefined NSS independently of use, measuring it simply on the basis of whether a woman thought she could have more children. This definition substantially increased the implied fecundity of the population. In Sri Lanka the mean NSS value increased from 67 to 84 percent; in Colombia, from 76 to 95 percent. Tables 4A.7 and 4A.8 report the proximate determinants and use equations with both the present and alternative definitions of NSS. As can be seen, although there are some changes in numerical magnitudes the results are basically the same. Of special note the conclusion about the importance of motivation in determining use (table 4A.8) is clearly not the product of the definition of NSS—note that the t-statistic on $Cn - Cd$ is virtually unchanged.

As a second test, we reran the use equation reported in the text (table 4.9) for all ever users of fertility control, confining the population to current regulators only. In this analysis we used the present definition of NSS, but since, by this definition, all current regulators have a value of one, NSS cannot explain differences in use. The results for current regulators look very much like those for all regulators (table 4A.9). Again, the conclusion is that the definition of NSS cannot account for our results. We preferred to use the present measure of NSS in chapter 4, because it yields more plausible average magnitudes of secondary sterility.

A second issue of possible bias—in this case with respect to the proximate determinants equation—arises because the denominator of the child mortality variable X_7, is the dependent variable, children

Table 4A.4 Second-stage Regression Results for Children Ever Born (Proximate Determinants) Equation with Varying Definitions of Use and Estimation Procedure, Continuously Married Females Aged 35–44, All Parities

Country and variable	Regression coefficient (standard error in parentheses)				Mean	Standard deviation
	U = Years since first use of fertility control			U = Ever used		
	Present method	2SLS	OLS	Logit/OLS		
A. Sri Lanka						
B, Children ever born	—	—	—	—	5.32	2.84
U, Use of fertility control	-.2899* (.0212)	-.4527* (.0312)	-.1104* (.0076)	-2.9164* (.3000)	4.06[a]	5.72[a]
X_1, Duration of marriage, years	.3235* (.0085)	.3703* (.0117)	.3087* (.0072)	.2857* (.0084)	19.41	6.11
X_2, First birth interval, months	-.0248* (.0013)	-.0278* (.0017)	-.0222* (.0011)	-.0241* (.0014)	27.95	38.50
X_3, Second birth interval, months	-.0282* (.0016)	-.0314* (.0020)	-.0261* (.0014)	-.0285* (.0017)	32.42	30.55
X_4, Not secondarily sterile (= 1; others = 0)	2.2367* (.1260)	2.7941* (.1687)	1.6253* (.0928)	2.6688* (.1821)	.64	.48
X_5, Months breastfeeding in last closed interval	-.0026* (.0038)	-.0212* (.0048)	-.0151* (.0033)	-.0244* (.0041)	17.03	12.73
X_6, Proportion of pregnancy wastage	-1.2151* (.3184)	-.6354 (.4085)	-1.5967* (.2737)	-1.3501* (.3297)	.07	.16
X_7, Proportion of child mortality	.3633 (.3275)	1.0462* (.4098)	1.1002* (.2803)	.7393* (.3355)	.08	.15
Constant	.7402	.3013	.4778	1.6531		
Number of cases	1796	1796	1796	1796		
$\bar{R}^2$	.52	.47	.64	.49		

B. Colombia

					Mean	SD
B, Children ever born	—	—	—	—	6.23	3.47
U, Use of fertility control	−.2532* (.0316)	−.3501* (.0399)	−.1572* (.0144)	−3.3350* (.5747)	6.44[a]	6.53[a]
X_1, Duration of marriage, years	.4368* (.0175)	.4788* (.0209)	.4194* (.0154)	.3885* (.0176)	18.97	5.84
X_2, First birth interval, months	−.0297* (.0027)	−.0329* (.0030)	−.0281* (.0025)	−.0309* (.0031)	21.51	34.50
X_3, Second birth interval, months	−.0337* (.0033)	−.0385* (.0038)	−.0327* (.0031)	−.0342* (.0039)	27.62	28.06
X_4, Not secondarily sterile (= 1; others = 0)	2.6927* (.2376)	2.8789* (.2605)	2.3158* (.2084)	2.9723* (.3101)	.75	.44
X_5, Months breastfeeding in last closed interval	−.0492* (.0126)	−.0639* (.0140)	−.0318* (.0111)	−.0437* (.0144)	8.80	7.88
X_6, Proportion of pregnancy wastage	−1.4815* (.6857)	−.7628 (.7592)	−1.3633* (.6598)	−.9077 (.7925)	.07	.13
X_7, Proportion of child mortality	1.9641* (.5188)	1.7681* (.5642)	2.6295* (.4758)	1.6906* (.6211)	.11	.18
Constant	−.6617	−.5515	−.8451	.6124		
Number of cases	628	628	628	628		
$\bar{R}^2$	.61	.58	.64	.50		

*Significant at .05 level or better; adjusted standard errors are shown.

[a] For ever used, the mean and standard deviation for Sri Lanka are, respectively, .53 and .50; for Colombia, .63 and .48.

Table 4A.5 First-stage Regression Results for Children Ever Born (Proximate Determinants) Equation with Varying Definitions of Use and Estimation Procedure, Continuously Married Females Aged 35–44, All Parities

Country and variable	Regression coefficient (standard error in parentheses)				
	U = Years since first use of fertility control		U = Ever used		Standard deviation
	Present method	2SLS	Logit/OLS	Mean	
A. Sri Lanka					
U	—	—	—	4.06[a]	5.72[a]
$X_1 (1-X_7)$	.6732*	.3689*	.0643*	17.66	5.99
	(.0529)	(.0252)	(.0136)		
$X_2 (1-X_7)$	−.0874*	−.0220*	−.0156*	25.96	38.04
	(.0122)	(.0034)	(.0030)		
$X_3 (1-X_7)$	−.0993*	−.0265*	−.0215*	29.78	29.30
	(.0148)	(.0044)	(.0039)		
$X_4 (1-X_7)$	8.8329*	3.7602*	2.7245*	.59	.46
	(.5690)	(.2934)	(.1609)		
$X_5 (1-X_7)$	−.0432*	−.0128	−.0205*	15.86	11.98
	(.0206)	(.0106)	(.0055)		
$X_6 (1-X_7)$	6.0096*	2.2053*	1.4505*	.06	.15
	(1.9022)	(.8387)	(.4980)		
X_7	6.0226	8.8384*	1.3436	.08	.15
	(3.3829)	(1.7319)	(.8648)		
X_7^2	1.6975	−4.8063	−1.3449	.03	.09
	(6.0570)	(2.8531)	(1.4279)		
Cd	−1.4313*	−.7901*	−.2190*	4.45	2.12
	(.1335)	(.0675)	(.0345)		
RC	1.7094*	.7281*	.5524*	2.01	1.55
	(.1587)	(.0822)	(.0470)		
Constant	−10.3732	−1.7831	−1.6302		
Number of cases	1796	1796	1796		
χ^2	682	—	826		
$\bar{R}^2$	—	.24	—		

Table 4A.5 Continued

Country and variable	Regression coefficient (standard error in parentheses)				
	$U =$ Years since first use of fertility control		$U =$ Ever used		Standard deviation
	Present method	2SLS	Logit/OLS	Mean	
B. Colombia					
U	—	—	—	6.44[a]	6.53[a]
$X_1 (1\text{-}X_7)$	.5780*	.4088*	.0603*	16.74	5.95
	(.0705)	(.0427)	(.0212)		
$X_2 (1\text{-}X_7)$	−.0966*	−.0258*	−.0242*	19.40	34.25
	(.0242)	(.0066)	(.0071)		
$X_3 (1\text{-}X_7)$	−.1017*	−.0443*	−.0224*	24.31	25.14
	(.0208)	(.0094)	(.0062)		
$X_4 (1\text{-}X_7)$	5.7929*	3.2234*	2.2555*	.72	.45
	(.8383)	(.5828)	(.2780)		
$X_5 (1\text{-}X_7)$	−.1979*	−.1180*	−.0464*	7.96	7.44
	(.0498)	(.0312)	(.0153)		
$X_6 (1\text{-}X_7)$	8.1765*	4.4911*	2.9434*	.02	.14
	(2.8632)	(1.8741)	(.9896)		
X_7	1.5165	5.1968	−.6314	.11	.18
	(4.3304)	(2.8497)	(1.3004)		
X_7^2	4.3291	.2563	.5572	.04	.12
	(6.6063)	(3.9489)	(1.8587)		
Cd	−.5630*	−.4048*	−.0915*	4.66	3.03
	(.1184)	(.0744)	(.0339)		
RC	1.2918	.7453*	.3596*	4.31	2.54
	(1.4230)	(.0893)	(.0468)		
Constant	−8.1032	−2.2340	−1.7102		
Number of cases	628	628	628		
χ^2	300	—	255		
$\bar{R}^2$	—	.32	—		

*Significant at .05 level or better.
[a]For ever use, the mean and standard deviation for Sri Lanka are, respectively, .53 and .50; for Colombia, .63 and .48.

Table 4A.6 Regression Results for Determinants of Use Equation with Varying Definitions of Use and Estimation Procedure, Continuously Married Females Aged 35–44, All Parities

	Regression coefficient (standard error in parentheses)				Mean (standard deviation in parentheses)			
	$U =$ Years since first use of fertility control			$U =$ Ever used	$U =$ Years since first use of fertility control			$U =$ Ever used
Country and variable	Present method	2SLS	OLS	Logit/OLS	Present method	2SLS	OLS	Logit/OLS
A. Sri Lanka								
Use of fertility control	—	—	—	—	4.06 (5.72)	4.06 (5.72)	4.06 (5.72)	.53 (.50)
Cn-Cd	1.9495* (.1690)	.8892* (.0491)	.9421* (.0586)	.3592* (.0273)	1.37 (2.26)	2.03 (2.47)	.76 (2.10)	1.77 (2.30)
Number of methods known	2.0283* (.2257)	.7320* (.0783)	.7814* (.0794)	.5991* (.0422)	2.01 (1.55)	2.01 (1.55)	2.01 (1.55)	2.01 (1.55)
Constant	-7.2965	.7822	1.7739	-1.6824				
Number of cases	1796	1796	1796	1796				
$\bar{R}^2$	—	.21	.18	—				
χ^2	492	—	—	537				

B. Colombia

Use of fertility control	—	—	—	—	6.44 (6.53)	6.44 (6.53)	6.44 (6.53)	.63 (.48)
$Cn\text{-}Cd$	.8627* (.1439)	.6277* (.0553)	.6537* (.0607)	.2041* (.0271)	2.10 (3.91)	2.77 (4.09)	1.64 (3.74)	2.64 (3.92)
Number of methods known	1.3643* (.2148)	.7274* (.0891)	.7547* (.0896)	.3266* (.0408)	4.31 (2.54)	4.31 (2.54)	4.31 (2.54)	4.31 (2.54)
Constant	-3.4106	1.5713	2.1183	-1.2827				
Number of cases	628	628	628	628				
$\bar{R}^2$	—	.27	.26	—				
χ^2	214	—	—	162				

*Significant at .05 level or better.

ever born. To test whether our results were affected by this, we reran the proximate determinants and use equations, deleting the X_7 term from the proximate determinants equation. As can be seen from tables 4A.10 and 4A.11, the results are virtually unchanged when X_7 is dropped. Hence, our conclusions do not depend on our inclusion of the child mortality variable.

Table 4A.7 Second-stage Regression Results for Children Ever Born (Proximate Determinants) Equation with Present and Alternative Definition of NSS, Continuously Married Females Aged 35–44, Parities Two and Higher

	Regression coefficient (standard error in parentheses)			
	Sri Lanka		Colombia	
Variable	Present NSS	Alternative NSS[a]	Present NSS	Alternative NSS[a]
U, Use of fertility control	−.3383*	−.2854*	−.2989*	−.2636*
	(.0257)	(.0264)	(.0361)	(.0401)
X_1, Duration of marriage, years	.3346*	.2973*	.4809*	.4196*
	(.0107)	(.0107)	(.0232)	(.0242)
X_2, First birth interval, months	−.0324*	−.0274*	−.0482*	−.0452*
	(.0029)	(.0029)	(.0076)	(.0084)
X_3, Second birth interval, months	−.0413*	−.0469*	−.0494*	−.0565*
	(.0029)	(.0031)	(.0070)	(.0079)
X_4, Not secondarily sterile ($= 1$; others $= 0$)	2.6211*	1.4578*	3.1637*	1.1328*
	(.1509)	(.1770)	(.2880)	(.5101)
X_5, Months of breastfeeding in last closed interval	−.0241*	−.0147*	−.0597*	−.0503*
	(.0044)	(.0046)	(.0153)	(.0169)
X_6, Proportion of pregnancy wastage	−1.5966*	−2.6737*	−1.0605	−1.1918
	(.4820)	(.4799)	(.8924)	(.9449)
X_7, Proportion of child mortality	.2842	.7251	2.3383*	1.6674*
	(.3854)	(.3881)	(.6194)	(.7046)
Constant	1.0296	2.0565	−.8217	1.7081
Number of cases	1608	1577	507	507
$\bar{R}^2$	.31	.28	.51	.39

*Significant at .05 level or better; adjusted standard errors are shown.
[a]The alternative definition is self-reported fecundity impairment. The mean and standard deviation for Sri Lanka are .84 and .37; for Colombia, .95 and .22.

Table 4A.8 Regression Results for Determinants of Use Equation with Present and Alternative Definition of *NSS*, Continuously Married Females Aged 35–44, Parities Two and Higher

	Regression coefficient (standard error in parentheses)			
	Sri Lanka		Colombia	
Variable	Present *NSS*	Alternative *NSS*[a]	Present *NSS*	Alternative *NSS*[a]
Cn-Cd	1.7534*	1.3791*	.9496*	.7780*
	(.1673)	(.1221)	(.1426)	(.1055)
Number of methods known	1.9761*	1.8237*	.9310*	1.3050*
	(.2278)	(.1598)	(.2186)	(.1525)
Constant	−6.8214	−5.3054	−1.2556	−2.3740
Number of cases	1608	1577	507	507
χ^2	382	276	158	134

*Significant at .05 level or better.
[a]See table 4A.7, note a.

Table 4A.9 Regression Results for Determinants of Use Equation for All Regulators and Current Regulators Only, Present Definition of *NSS*, Continuously Married Females Aged 35–44, Parities Two and Higher

	Regression coefficient (standard error in parentheses)			
	Sri Lanka		Colombia	
Variable	All regulators	Current regulators	All regulators	Current regulators
Cn-Cd	1.3349*	1.6623*	.6425*	.7878*
	(.1570)	(.2051)	(.0872)	(.1076)
Number of methods known	−.3074	−.2148	.2258	.2470
	(.2048)	(.2368)	(.1500)	(.1724)
Constant	4.2260	2.0706	6.8413	6.0987
Number of cases	898	660	352	262
χ^2	88	80	52	55

*Significant at .05 level or better.

Table 4A.10 Second-stage Regression Results for Children Ever Born (Proximate Determinants) Equation with Child Mortality Variable Included and Excluded, Continuously Married Females Aged 35–44, Parities Two and Higher

	Regression coefficient (standard error in parentheses)			
	Sri Lanka		Colombia	
	Child mortality		Child mortality	
Variable	Included	Excluded	Included	Excluded
U, Use of fertility	−.3383*	−.3425*	−.2989*	−.3480*
control	(.0257)	(.0251)	(.0361)	(.0363)
X_1, duration of marriage,	.3346*	.3236*	.4809*	.4813*
years	(.0107)	(.0104)	(.0232)	(.0231)
X_2, First birth interval,	−.0324*	−.0316*	−.0482*	−.0491*
months	(.0029)	(.0029)	(.0076)	(.0081)
X_3, Second birth interval,	−.0413*	−.0456*	−.0494*	−.0588*
months	(.0029)	(.0030)	(.0070)	(.0074)
X_4, Not secondarily sterile	2.6211*	2.5776*	3.1637*	3.1787*
(= 1; others = 0)	(.1509)	(.1519)	(.2880)	(.2987)
X_5, Months breastfeeding in	−.0242*	−.0216*	−.0597*	−.0745*
last closed interval	(.0044)	(.0045)	(.0153)	(.0160)
X_6, Proportion of	−1.5966*	−2.0425*	−1.0605	.1422
pregnancy wastage	(.4820)	(.4738)	(.8924)	(.9059)
X_7, Proportion of child	.2842	—	2.3383*	—
mortality	(.3854)		(.6194)	
Constant	1.0296	1.4805	−.8217	.1344
Number of cases	1608	1577	507	507
$\bar{R}^2$	.31	.30	.51	.44

*Significant at .05 level or better; adjusted standard errors are shown.

Table 4A.11 Regression Results for Determinants of Use Equation with Child Mortality Variable Included and Excluded, Continuously Married Females Aged 35–44, Parities Two and Higher

	Regression coefficient (standard error in parentheses)			
	Sri Lanka		Colombia	
	Child mortality		Child mortality	
Variable	Included	Excluded	Included	Excluded
Cn-Cd	1.7534*	1.7111*	.9496*	.8844*
	(.1673)	(.1130)	(.1426)	(.0966)
Number of methods known	1.9761*	1.5986*	.9310*	1.2331*
	(.2278)	(.1556)	(.2186)	(.1485)
Constant	− 6.8214	− 5.7648	− 1.2556	− 2.8598
Number of cases	1608	1577	507	507
χ^2	382	378	158	162

*Significant at .05 level or better.

III
Macro Studies

5
The Historical Experience of Karnataka and Taiwan

With K. Srinivasan and Shireen J. Jejeebhoy

In this and the following chapter, the analysis shifts from the micro to the macro level, first with a time series study, then with a cross-sectional analysis. As in the preceding chapters, the emphasis in these two chapters is on links from demand, supply, and regulation costs to fertility control and fertility.

In 1951 the United Nations Population Division and Government of India conducted jointly the Mysore Population Study, a survey of fertility and family planning practices under essentially premodern conditions, a survey widely acclaimed for its pioneering scope and exceptional quality (United Nations 1961). In 1975, the Bangalore Population Institute, under its director, K. Srinivasan, conducted a similar survey of fairly comparable scope, the Bangalore Population Study (Srinivasan, Reddy, and Raju 1977). These surveys of what is now the Indian state of Karnataka, plus several fairly similar historical surveys for Taiwan, provide a unique opportunity for examining questions such as the following about supply, demand, and regulation costs in the early phase of the transition from natural fertility to deliberate fertility control: In an early modern or premodern situation, is the typical household likely to have more children than it wants if it does nothing deliberately to restrict fertility? Or does its supply of children equal or fall short of demand, so that there is a lack of motivation for fertility control? Are regulation costs high, discouraging deliberate control? As modernization progresses does the motivation for control rise, and, if so, is this due to the trend in supply, demand, or both? Do regulation costs decline? What are the relative weights of motivation and costs of regulation in inducing deliberate fertility control? To what extent is increasing fertility control accompanied by actual fertility decline? And what of trends in fertility differentials during the transition—are there systematic shifts in differentials by age or socioeconomic status?

In addition to these general questions, the analysis also enables us to form a tentative impression on an important substantive issue. There is a widespread impression that India's progress in adopting fertility control and achieving fertility reduction has been disappointing. The present theoretical framework makes possible a formal assessment of this view, by comparing Karnataka's experience with Taiwan's, an area of about the same size population as Karnataka.

In what follows, we take up the experience of Karnataka first and then turn to the comparison with Taiwan. The analysis of trends in fertility differentials comes last.

Karnataka

Data and Methods

Although generally similar, there are a number of differences between the Mysore Population Study (MPS) and the Bangalore Population Study (BPS) in purpose, definitions, population coverage, and geographic scope. (For a discussion, see Srinivasan, Reddy, and Raju 1978, p. 259; 1977, pp. 3–9.) An attempt has been made to select the most comparable data for the present purpose and, if possible, to adjust for discrepancies, but the options were limited. In addition, consistency with the other chapters in this volume was an objective. Details regarding sources and methods are given in the notes to the tables. What follows is a summary of the scope, the measures used, and some of the principal conceptual and empirical deficiencies.

The study population is, principally, continuously married females aged 35–44. For 1975, however, data for currently married females had to be taken as equal to those for continuously married; moreover, for 1951, the actual age span sometimes differs among measures. The urban data for both dates are for the city of Bangalore, the largest city in Karnataka; the rural data for 1951 are for "rural plains," for 1975 for "all rural," which is fairly comparable in geographic scope to "rural plains" in 1951.

The principal variables in the analysis are as follows:

1. Fertility (B) is measured in terms of the mean number of births per continuously married woman. Surviving children (C) is the product of fertility (B) and the child survival ratio (s).

2. Fertility control (U) is based on ever used contraception (including abstinence) or contraceptive sterilization. Induced abortion is not included, for lack of data.

3. Costs of regulation (RC) is estimated as the mean number of fertility control methods known per couple, costs of control being assumed to vary inversely with methods known. Methods known excludes abstinence, which was omitted from survey questions on knowledge (but not use), and is based on reports of knowledge after respondents were read a list of methods, i.e., it is knowledge after prompting.

4. Demand (Cd) is measured somewhat differently in the two surveys: "In the Mysore Population Study, each woman was asked the ideal number of children a couple should have, without any reference to the number of children the respondent had at the time of the survey. In the Bangalore Population Study, each woman was asked the number of additional children she would like to have, and this figure was added to the number she had at the time of the survey to obtain the desired family size. The latter procedure can be expected to give a higher value than the former, since a woman cannot desire a family size that is smaller than she has already; this may not be the case according to the procedure adopted in the Mysore Population Study. It should also be noted that in the MPS husbands and wives in the same selected households were interviewed, whereas in the BPS husbands and wives in alternate households were interviewed" (Srinivasan, Reddy, and Raju 1978, p. 265). The ages covered by the demand measures include younger couples as well as older, but the 1951 survey reports that there is little correlation of desired family size with age (United Nations 1961, 141).

5. Supply (Cn) is the product of natural fertility (N) and the child survival ratio (s). Natural fertility (N) is the mean number of births per continuously married woman that would have occurred in the absence of deliberate family size limitation. It is obtained as the sum of two components: (a) for females 20–39 the Coale-Trussell standard value of natural fertility for each five-year age group (Coale and Trussell 1975b) is multiplied by five and then adjusted downward by the Coale-Trussell scale factor, M (Coale and Trussell 1974), as estimated for each geographic area from the age-specific marital fertility rates by five-year age groups of females 15–44; (b) for females aged

15–19, the observed marital fertility rate was taken as the natural fertility rate and multiplied by 3, the assumed average number of years' exposure in that age bracket, except for Bangalore in 1975, when the multiplier was 1.5. As shown in Crimmins and Easterlin (1984), this technique of estimating natural fertility yields quite similar orders of magnitude at the macro level to a number of alternatives not possible with these data.

The analysis throughout is based on averages for the population, a choice necessitated by the data; individual households would, of course, show considerable variability about the mean.

Empirical Results

Although the data are imperfect, they give a coherent and informative picture when pieced together in terms of the theoretical framework. First, with regard to the supply of children, they indicate that in Karnataka in 1951, if a husband and wife were continuously married and did nothing to limit their fertility, they would have had, on the average, about 4.3 surviving children by the end of the wife's

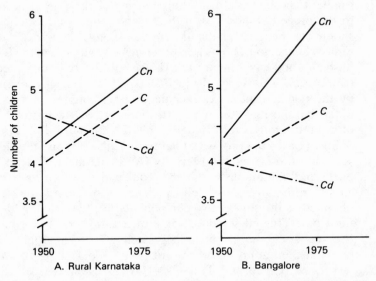

Fig. 5.1 Supply (*Cn*), Demand (*Cd*), and Number of Surviving Children (*C*), Women Aged 35–44 in Rural Karnataka and Bangalore, 1951 and 1975. Source: Tables 5.2 and 5.5.

reproductive career (fig. 5.1 and table 5.1, col. 3). The typical couple's fertility would have been considerably higher—on the order of 6 births per wife—but high infant and child mortality would have reduced the survivors to about 70 percent of this figure (cols. 1 and 2). By 1975, the supply of children would have averaged almost one-fourth greater in rural areas and over one-third greater in urban (col. 3). This growth in supply was partly due to an improvement in child survival rates, which occurred at about the same pace in rural as in urban areas (col. 2). It was also due to increased natural fertility. In urban areas the contribution of natural fertility to raising supply was just about the same as that of improved child survival; in rural areas, the contribution, though positive, was considerably less. Subsequently, in the discussion of table 5.4, we shall see that the 1951 rural natural fertility estimate is probably overstated; hence, the increase in rural natural fertility is probably understated and, in actuality, more like the urban increase.

To turn to the demand for children, in 1951 the number of children desired averaged 4.0 in urban areas and 4.6 in rural (fig. 5.1 and table 5.2, col. 2) Subsequently, demand trended downward, and by about the same amount in both rural and urban areas. Because of this, an

Table 5.1 Natural Fertility, Child Survival Ratio, and Potential Supply, Women 35–44 in Rural Karnataka and Bangalore, 1951 and 1975

	(1) Natural fertility, N	(2) Survival ratio, s	(3) Potential supply, Cn
A. Rural Karnataka			
1951	6.27	.686	4.30
1975	6.58	.798	5.25
% change (1951–75)	4.9	16.3	22.1
B. Bangalore			
1951	5.94	.739	4.39
1975	6.85	.865	5.93
% change (1951–75)	15.3	17.1	35.1

Sources and methods: Col. 1: see text for method used; age-specific marital fertility rates used to derive the Coale-Trussell value of M are from Srinivasan, Reddy, and Raju 1978, p. 261; the standard rates of natural fertility for ages 20–39 are from A. J. Coale and J. Trussell (1975a). The estimate of M was based on a program covering ages 15–44 developed at the International Institute of Population Studies under the supervision of Jejeebhoy and Srinivasan. Col. 2: data for 1951 from United Nations 1961, p. 114; for 1975 and from Srinivasan, Reddy, and Raju 1977, p. 47. Col. 3: col. 1 × col. 2.

Table 5.2 Potential Supply, Demand, and Motivation for Fertility Control of Women 35–44 in Rural Karnataka and Bangalore, 1951 and 1975

	(1)	(2)	(3)
			Motivation for
	Supply,	Demand,	fertility control,
	Cn	Cd	$Cn-Cd$
A. Rural Karnataka			
1951	4.30	4.65	−.35
1975	5.25	4.20	1.05
Change (1951–75)	.95	−.45	1.40
B. Bangalore			
1951	4.39	4.00	.39
1975	5.93	3.70	2.23
Change (1951–75)	1.54	−.30	1.84

Sources and methods: Col. 1: table 5.1, col. 3, col. 2: for 1951, rural figure (average of wives 18–33 and their husbands) and urban (average of wives 30–33 and husbands 36 +), from United Nations 1961, pp. 140–41. For 1975, from Srinivasan, Reddy, and Raju 1977, p. 49 (average of females 15–44 and their husbands). Col. 3: col. 1 − col. 2.

initial excess of rural over urban demand for children persisted throughout the period. The size of the decline in demand shown here is probably somewhat understated, because of the change in concept noted above.

Comparing demand with supply, one finds that in rural areas in 1951 supply fell short of demand by about 0.4 children (fig. 5.1 and table 5.2, col. 3). This means that the typical married couple was unable to have as many children as were wanted, even if the spouses enjoyed an unbroken marriage throughout the wife's reproductive career and did nothing to limit their fertility. To be sure, this is an average situation—some couples had as many as or more children than they desired, while others had a much greater shortfall. And in urban areas the situation was the opposite of the rural—on the average, supply exceeded demand by about 0.4 children. The rural sector, however, was typical of India at this time; hence, the representative family situation in India in 1951 may well have been one where couples had difficulty in achieving their family size desires even under the best of circumstances.

By 1975, the situation had changed dramatically. As has been noted, in both rural and urban areas supply trended upward over the period while demand moved downward. In rural areas the shortfall of supply compared with demand was replaced by an excess, amounting to about one child; in urban areas, the modest initial excess of 0.4

children rose to 2.2. By 1975, therefore, in both rural and urban areas unregulated fertility was likely to result in more children than were wanted.

The trends in both supply and demand contributed to this rise in the potential number of unwanted children, but of the two, the trend in supply seemingly made a more important contribution, accounting for two-thirds or more of the growth (fig. 5.1 and table 5.2, lines 3 and 6). As has been seen, the rising trend in supply was, in turn, due to increases in both child survival and natural fertility rates. Thus, it appears that in this period enhanced child survival and natural fertility, more than a changing demand for children, were chiefly responsible for pushing families into a potential excess supply situation. Allowance for the probable understatement in the decline of demand would, however, improve the relative showing of demand.

At both dates, urban couples tended toward an excess supply of children much more than did rural, because of both lower demand and higher supply. Comparing the contributions to this excess of the differences in demand and supply, one finds that in 1951 the difference in demand was more important than that in supply; by 1975 the contributions from demand and supply were roughly equal. This cross-sectional pattern is fairly similar to that of chapter 4, where demand and supply were found to be about equally important in accounting for point-of-time differences in household motivation.

To turn to use of control, one would expect that if couples could not have as many childen as they wanted even if fertility were unregulated, as in rural areas in 1951, then the use of control would be quite limited. This, indeed, proves to be the case; in rural areas at this time, fertility control was almost nonexistent (table 5.3, cols. 1 and 3). (The fact that there was some fertility control even though the average situation was one of excess demand for children reflects the fact that some couples were considerably above the average, in an excess supply situation.) If rural Karnataka in 1951 is representative of premodern or early modern situations more generally, then this implies that the absence of deliberate control in such situations—that is, the prevalence of a "natural fertility" regime—is due to lack of motivation—an inability of most couples to produce as many surviving children as they would like to have.

In urban areas in 1951, the average level of motivation was, as noted, slightly positive. Correspondingly, there was somewhat higher use of control than in rural areas, though use was still low.

One would expect that the appearance and growth of a potential

Table 5.3 Motivation for Fertility Control and Costs of Regulation for Women 35–44, and Percent of Women 20–39 and 35–39 Controlling Fertility, Rural Karnataka and Bangalore, 1951 and 1975

	(1) Motivation for fertility control, Cn-Cd	(2) Costs of regulation, RC	(3) Percent controlling U (20–39)	(4) Percent controlling U (35–39)
A. Rural Karnataka				
1951	−.35	0.3	3.4	n.a.
1975	1.05	2.9	21.0	25.6
B. Bangalore				
1951	.39	0.8	15.3	22.2
1975	2.23	2.3	36.0	48.6

n.a. = not available

Sources and methods: Col. 1: table 5.2, col. 3. Col. 2: for Bangalore, estimated from Srinivasan, Reddy, and Raju 1977, p. 55 (average for wives 30–34 and husbands 40 +); for rural, estimated for all reproductive ages from United Nations 1961, pp. 161–62 and Srinivasan, Reddy, and Raju 1977, pp. 54–55; older couples were assumed to deviate from the average to the same extent as in urban areas, as shown in Srinivasan, Reddy, and Raju 1977, p. 55. Col. 3: rural figure for 1951 is from United Nations 1961, pp. 167–68 (weighted average of couples with wife 20–33 and 34–39); for 1975, figures are estimates for couples with wife 20–39 based on unpublished age-specific data from Srinivasan, Reddy, and Raju 1977. Col. 4: for 1951, Bangalore figure is from United Nations 1961, p. 168 (couples with wife 30–33); for 1975, from unpublished data for females 35–39 from Srinivasan, Reddy, and Raju 1977.

surplus of children would induce a growing motivation for control and thereby increase use. Again, this is the case. In both rural and urban areas, increasing motivation was accompanied by increased fertility regulation (col. 3).

Motivation is, of course, only one factor determining the use of control; the other is the costs of fertility regulation, both subjective and objective. It is possible that greater use could also result from lower costs of regulation, once supply exceeds demand.

The measure of costs of regulation that is available for comparison over time—number of methods of control known—is far from the ideal, for reasons stated in chapter 3. The measure does show, however, a growth in knowledge over the period (that is, reduced costs of regulation), and thus a trend that would contribute to greater use of control (col. 2). Moreover, it shows a very low level of knowledge at the start of the period, which again would be consistent with the low use of control at that time. Moreover, among those reporting knowledge, sterilization, which is likely to be viewed as having serious drawbacks, is by far the leading method (United Nations 1961, p. 162). In general, then, costs of regulation as well as motivation, appear to have contributed to both low initial use and the growth in use over time.

Given the imperfections in the present measures of motivation and costs of regulation and the small number of observations, an assessment of the relative importance of the two in inducing fertility control is difficult. However, the data do offer one suggestion that motivation was more important than costs. This appears when one seeks to account for the consistent excess of urban over rural areas in the use of control. On this, the motivation measure indicates that more motivation existed in urban areas at both dates. The situation regarding regulation costs, however, favored higher use in urban areas only at the start of the period. Based on costs of regulation alone, one would have expected rural areas to have greater use than urban at the end of the period, a situation contrary to fact. Thus, in 1975 the rural-urban difference in use of control was not consistent with that in costs of regulation, implying that higher motivation in urban areas must have been the dominant factor.

It is unusual to observe more rapid growth of contraceptive knowledge in rural than urban areas, and rural knowledge greater than urban, as in Karnataka in 1975. The explanation is the special nature of the Indian family planning program, "that mass sterilization camps . . . [were] conducted in rural areas in large numbers since 1965 and the sterilization programmes were more well known to the population in the rural areas than in the urban areas" (Srinivasan, Reddy, and Raju 1977, p. 25). An implication of the present analysis—again subject to the caution about imperfections of the measures—is that the emphasis of the program on rural over urban areas may have been misplaced, because in rural areas the program was more handicapped by lack of motivation than it would have been in urban areas.

Despite the increase from 1951 to 1975 in the proportion of the population seeking deliberately to limit family size, the number of births per woman either rose, as in rural areas, or remained constant, as in urban (table 5.4, cols. 1–3). This does not mean that fertility control was ineffective. As has been seen, natural fertility was rising during this period. The growth in fertility control, while not enough to reduce the absolute number of births per woman, did serve to moderate the increase. This is clearest for the urban sector. By subtracting actual from natural fertility, one obtains an estimate of births averted (col. 5). The rise in urban fertility control from 1951 to 1975 reduced

Table 5.4 Percent of Women 20–39 and 35–39 Controlling Fertility, and Children Ever Born, Natural Fertility, and Births Averted for Women 35–44 in Rural Karnataka and Bangalore, 1951 and 1975

	(1)	(2)	(3)	(4)	(5)
	Percent controlling		Children ever born,	Natural fertility,	Births averted,
	U (20–39)	U (35–39)	B	N	N-B
A. Rural Karnataka					
1951	3.4	n.a.	5.90	6.27	.37
1975	21.0	25.6	6.20	6.58	.38
B. Bangalore					
1951	15.3	22.2	5.40	5.94	.54
1975	36.0	48.6	5.40	6.85	1.45

n.a. = not available

Sources and methods: Cols. 1 and 2: table 5.3, cols. 3 and 4. Col. 3: for 1951, urban figure is from United Nations 1961, p. 115, and rural figure is from United Nations 1961, p. 112, adjusted upward by 0.8, the excess of children ever born for continuously married over all wives (p. 115); for 1975, figure for all ever-married women in Srinivasan, Reddy, and Raju 1977, p. 45, was increased by 0.4 in rural sector and 0.2 in urban sector to obtain estimate for continuously married wives. Col. 4: table 5.1, col. 1. Col. 5: col. 4 − col. 3.

potential fertility, on the average, by about one birth; in other words, whereas fertility control in 1951 averted about 0.5 births, by 1975 it averted almost 1.5 births. For the rural sector, there is little indication that increased use raised the number of births averted, but it seems likely that this result arises from an overestimate of rural natural fertility in 1951. As we have seen, fertility control was negligible in rural areas; hence it is likely that potential fertility was much closer to the observed level of 5.9 births per woman than the present natural fertility estimate indicates. If this were true, then the rural trend in births averted would be positive, like the urban.

The most important point is that a rise in observed fertility should not be taken to mean that the fertility transition is not underway or that fertility control is ineffective. As has been seen, in Karnataka during this period supply-demand pressures developed, inducing greater regulation of fertility, and the population responded to these pressures with a sizable increase in use of control. The increase in use resulted in more births averted (this is clearly so in the urban sector, and probably so in the rural) but the tendency of this to reduce fertility was defeated by an even greater rise in natural fertility.

These observations may also explain the seeming contradiction between the movement in the demand for children and that in actual fertility. As has been seen, the number of births per woman rose, despite a downward trend in desired family size. (Observations such as this have led some to despair of the meaningfulness of responses on desired size.) But the trend in desired family size was, in fact, having a negative impact on fertility via its contribution to motivating increased use of fertility control. This negative impact, however, was more than offset by the rise in natural fertility, yielding the seemingly inconsistent pattern of decreasing demand for children and rising births per woman.

As figure 5.1 shows, the rise in the use of fertility control was accompanied by a growth in the average number of surviving children per couple. This growth was even greater than that in births per woman (compare table 5.5, col. 1, with table 5.4, col. 3). In the case of surviving children per couple, the negative impact of increasing use of fertility control was countered, not only by rising natural fertility, but also by decreased child mortality. In 1951 in rural areas the average number of surviving children fell considerably short of that desired, while in urban areas the two magnitudes were equal (table 5.5, cols. 1–3). The increase in survivorship led by 1975 to a substantial excess of surviving children over desired family size—by 0.7 children in rural

Table 5.5 Surviving Children, Demand for Children, Unwanted Children and Potential Unwanted Children for Women 35–44 in Rural Karnataka and Bangalore, 1951 and 1975

	(1) Surviving children, C	(2) Demand, Cd	(3) Un- wanted children, C-Cd	(4) Potential unwanted children, Cn-Cd
A. Rural Karnataka				
1951	4.05	4.65	− .60	− .35
1975	4.90	4.20	.70	1.05
B. Bangalore				
1951	4.00	4.00	0.00	.39
1975	4.70	3.70	1.00	2.23

Sources and methods: Col. 1: obtained as product of children ever born and child survival ratio, as given in table 5.4, col. 3, and table 5.1, col. 2. Col. 2: table 5.2, col. 2. Col. 3: col. 1 − col. 2. Col. 4: table 5.2, col. 3.

areas and 1.0 in urban (col. 3). Thus, despite the growing use of fertility control, unwanted children became a more prevalent phenomenon. This, too, may be typical of an early stage of the fertility transition. Nevertheless, the mean number of unwanted children in 1975 was considerably smaller than that which would have occurred had fertility not been regulated at all; this is shown by comparison of the actual number of unwanted children with the potential number, the excess of supply over demand (cols. 3 and 4).

A Comparison of Karnataka and Taiwan

The Taiwan data come largely from Jejeebhoy's analysis (Jejeebhoy 1978, 1979). Since the Taiwan data are for continuously married wives aged 35–39, the Karnataka data have been similarly adjusted to age 35–39, though this is possible only for the year 1975. There are also a number of other differences. Natural fertility in Taiwan is estimated by a different technique, one that, compared with the technique used in the Karnataka analysis, tends to yield a slightly lower level of natural fertility. Also, the definition of desired family size (the number of surviving children a respondent would like to have had if she could start again) is more similar to that in Karnataka in 1951 than 1975. The measure of costs of regulation (number of methods known) includes abstinence in Taiwan; also the types of methods known differ in a way suggesting lower regulation costs in Taiwan (the IUD, the method emphasized in Taiwan, would most likely be viewed as having less serious drawbacks than sterilization, the method best known in India). Finally, the Taiwan analysis is not available for rural and urban areas separately, though such differences are usually small in Taiwan (Chang 1978). These differences between the analyses for Karnataka and Taiwan suggest that while there is interest in seeing how the experience of the two areas compares, the conclusions drawn cannot be taken without reservation.

This last statement does not apply, however, to observations based wholly on Taiwanese experience, and there the number of parallels with the findings for Karnataka is remarkable. The potential supply of children rises over the period due to increases in both natural fertility and child survival rates (figure 5.2 and table 5.6, panel A, cols. 1–3). Demand trends downward, though there is an initial period of stability (col. 4). The motivation for control, the excess of supply over demand, is low at the start of the period and rises steadily and markedly (col.5). Number of methods known rises slightly through 1965, and, thereafter

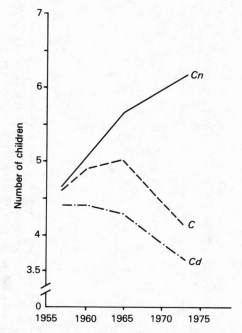

Fig. 5.2 Supply (*Cn*), Demand (*Cd*), and Number of Surviving Children (*C*), Women Aged 35–39 in Taiwan, 1957–73. Source: Table 5.6.

(in conjunction with a marked expansion in the family planning program) quite sharply. This implies a mild downward trend in fertility control costs before 1965, and thereafter a sharp drop. The use of fertility control rises noticeably both before and after 1965, presumably before 1965 due chiefly to growing motivation, thereafter, to both increased motivation and reduced fertility control costs (col. 7). The number of births per woman rises at first, despite the increase in fertility control, but then turns downward (col. 8). The number of surviving children rises more and for a longer period than births per woman, but also eventually turns downward (col. 9). Births averted trends steadily upward with the growing use of fertility control (col. 10). The excess of surviving children over desired family size, the number of unwanted children, rises for a while, despite the growing use of fertility control, but eventually turns downward (col. 11).

Note that the respects in which Taiwanese experience departs from

Table 5.6 Selected Fertility and Fertility Control Measures for Women 35–39 in Taiwan, Rural Karnataka, and Bangalore at Specified Dates

	(1) Natural fertility, N	(2) Survival rate, s	(3) Supply, C_n	(4) Demand, C_d	(5) Motivation for control, C_n-C_d	(6) Costs of regulation, RC	(7) Percent controlling, U	(8) Children ever born, B	(9) Children surviving, C	(10) Births averted, N-B	(11) Unwanted children, C-C_d
A. Taiwan											
1957	5.55	.843	4.68	4.40	.28	<3.0	12.0	5.46	4.60	.09	.20
1960	5.76	.874	5.03	4.39	.64	3.0	22.7	5.61	4.87	.15	.48
1965	6.27	.901	5.65	4.28	1.37	3.7	44.2	5.56	5.01	.61	.73
1973	6.31	.977	6.16	3.66	2.50	6.2	83.9	4.38	4.11	1.93	.45
B. Rural Karnataka											
1975	6.00	.764	4.58	4.20	.38	2.9	25.6	5.80	4.40	.20	.20
C. Bangalore											
1975	6.21	.875	5.43	3.70	1.73	2.3	48.6	5.00	4.40	1.21	.70

Sources and methods: For Taiwan, 1960–73 data are from Jejeebhoy 1979, pp. 89–90 (for col. 2 above), 94 (col. 4), 118 (col. 6), 206 (col. 7), 208 (col. 8), 219 (cols. 3 and 9). Col. 1 is the quotient of col. 3 divided by col. 2. For cols. 2, 4, and 6, the 1960 figure for women 35–39 was assumed equal to 1965 figure for women 40–44. For 1957, estimates are based chiefly on S. Chen 1963, pp. 209–94, except that for col. 6, where 1957 value is assumed to be lower than that for 1960. For Karnataka, cols. 2, 7, 8, and 9 are from unpublished data for females 35–39 underlying the published Srinivasan, Reddy, and Raju 1977. Col. 1 is obtained by adjusting the estimate in table 5.1, col. 1, for 2.5 years less exposure (the approximate difference between mean age of females 35–44 and that of females 35–39). Col. 4 is assumed to be the same as in table 5.2, col. 2, and col. 6, as in table 5.3, col. 2.

that of Karnataka—the eventual declines in births per woman, number of surviving children, and "unwanted" children—all occur at a time when, roughly speaking, more than half of the population is limiting family size, that is, at a stage in the transition to deliberate control later than that reached in Karnataka by 1975.

The Taiwan data underscore a point made in chapter 4 that the actual number of unwanted children $(C - Cd)$ is a poorer measure of the motivation for control than the potential number $(Cn - Cd)$ (cf. table 4.5). As just noted, as the transition progresses, the growing prevalence of fertility control leads to a downturn in the actual number of unwanted children. Thus, if one were to use the excess of the actual number of surviving children over the number wanted to infer the degree of motivation for control, one would eventually observe a period in which increasing control was seemingly accompanied by decreasing motivation. In contrast, the excess of supply over demand trends steadily upward, signifying growing motivation throughout the period. (Indeed, in a "perfect contraceptive society" [Bumpass and Westoff 1970] where there were no unwanted children, there would be the startling anomaly of zero motivation—by the measure of surviving children less desired family size—and universal use!)

The remaining comparisons of Karnataka and Taiwan are more tenuous, because the demands made on the accuracy of the underlying measures are greater. Nevertheless, they are of interest and further demonstrate the analytical potential of the theoretical framework.

There is, first, the oft-discussed issue of the responsiveness of the Indian population to fertility control—the complaint is sometimes raised that in India the population does not adopt family planning as rapidly as it "should." The theoretical framework here makes it possible to give analytical content to the meaning of "should"; specifically, the question is whether the adoption of fertility control in Karnataka is low for its level of motivation (the excess of supply over demand) and costs of regulation. To answer this, one can compare Karnataka's use of fertility control with that of Taiwan under comparable conditions of motivation and regulation costs. For this purpose a rough upward adjustment of methods known in Karnataka of 0.5 to 1.0 needs to be made, to allow for the omission of abstinence.

Turning first to the rural sector of Karnataka, one finds that in 1975 the level of motivation corresponded to that at a pre-1960 date in Taiwan, and number of methods known (including an upward adjustment for the omission of abstinence), to that at a post-1960 date (table 5.6, panels A and B, cols. 5 and 6). Taking the 1960 situation in

Taiwan, then, as roughly equivalent to the 1975 situation in rural
Karnataka, one finds that the use of fertility control is quite similar,
with the proportion of the population having ever used control in the
neighborhood of one-fourth (col. 7). With regard to the urban sector,
Karnataka in 1975 had a motivation measure corresponding to a
post-1965 date in Taiwan, but a regulation cost measure (again, including an upward adjustment for abstinence) corresponding to a pre-1965
situation. The actual prevalence of control, somewhat less than one-
half, was of the same order of magnitude as Taiwan's in 1965 (panels A
and C, cols. 5–7). Although this comparison may be pushing the data
too far, it suggests rather similar magnitudes of fertility control in
Karnataka and Taiwan under what seem to be roughly comparable
conditions of motivation and costs of regulation. If this finding is
correct, it implies that much of the disappointment over India's progress in the adoption of deliberate fertility control is unwarranted and
arises from failure to recognize the comparatively early stage of the
transition to fertility control in India.

A rough comparison of the two countries with regard to effectiveness of birth control is also possible. The proportion controlling fertility was about the same in rural Karnataka in 1975, urban Karnataka in
1951, and Taiwan in 1960 (table 5.7, col. 1). In the two Indian areas,
the mean number of births averted appears to have been as high as or
higher than in Taiwan (col. 2). Similarly, urban Karnataka in 1975 has
roughly the same proportion controlling as Taiwan in 1965, and the
Indian area has a larger number of births averted. However, births
averted in Taiwan may be somewhat understated relative to Karnataka, because, as noted previously, the technique used in estimating
natural fertility differs between the two areas in a way that might
produce a downward bias in Taiwan's natural fertility relative to
Karnataka's.

This problem should have less effect on comparisons of the two
areas with regard to changes over time. In urban Karnataka in 1951
and Taiwan in 1960, the proportion using control is about the same; in
Karnataka the *change* in this proportion between 1951 and 1975 is
slightly higher than that in Taiwan from 1960 to 1965; however, the
change in births averted is about double that in Taiwan (cols. 3 and 4).
The time series comparison thus points to the same conclusion as the
cross-sectional—greater effectiveness of fertility control in Karnataka
than Taiwan. Whether this is due to greater duration of use, more
effective methods, or both, is uncertain. However, as mentioned, the
Indian family planning program has stressed sterilization as the prin-

Table 5.7 Percent Controlling Fertility, Births Averted, and Change in Percent Controlling and Births Averted for Women 35–39 in Taiwan, Rural Karnataka, and Bangalore at Selected Dates

	Percent controlling, U	Births averted, N-B	Change from preceding date	
			Percent controlling, $\Delta(U)$	Births averted, $\Delta(N$-$B)$
A. Taiwan				
1957	12.0	.09	—	—
1960	22.7	.15	10.7	.06
1965	44.2	.71	21.5	.56
1973	83.9	1.93	39.7	1.22
B. Rural Karnataka				
1975	25.6	.20	—	—
C. Bangalore				
1951	22.2	n.a. *.54*[a]	—	—
1975	48.6	1.21 *1.45*	26.4	n.a. *.91*

[a]Figures in italics are for females 35–44.
n.a. = not available.
Sources: Table 5.6, except figures in italics, from table 5.4.

cipal method of fertility control, while the Taiwan program has stressed the IUD.

To judge from the Taiwan data, the effectiveness of fertility control tends to increase over time. In each successive period in Taiwan, the proportion controlling increased, and births averted rose at an even greater rate (table 5.7, cols. 3 and 4). It seems reasonable to suppose that as the proportion controlling increases, this is accompanied by greater length of use and increasing efficiency of use, and that this is what these data reflect.

The final comparison of experience in the two areas relates to the rate of progress in the motivation for fertility control. On this score, the data suggest that the motivation has been growing more slowly in India. In Taiwan, for example, the motivation for control rose by about 2.2 children in only 16 years, between 1957 and 1973 (table 5.6, col. 5). To take for comparison the urban sector of Karnataka, for which the trend data are the most reliable, after 24 years the level of motivation had risen, at best, by about 1.8 children (see the figures for females 35–44 in table 5.2, col. 3).

It seems likely that this difference in the growth of motivation for fertility control reflects the different pace of modernization in the two areas. As one indication, real per capita income growth in Taiwan from 1960 to 1975 was 5.9 percent per year; in India 0.8 percent per year (Morawetz 1977). Although the growth rate in urban Karnataka was probably higher than for India as a whole, it is doubtful that it approached that for Taiwan, which had one of the highest growth rates in the world during this period (Morawetz 1977).

While India's transition to deliberate control is occurring at a slower pace than Taiwan's, probably because of a corresponding difference in rates of modernization, it should also be noted that it is occurring at a lower level of modernization than Taiwan's. This is apparent from the relative income data, which put India at 17 percent of Taiwan's level in 1975 (Morawetz 1977), as well as from the child survival rates in tables 5.1 and 5.6, which show India to be considerably below Taiwan. The present theoretical framework suggests a possible reason for the earlier shift to deliberate control in Karnataka, namely, that the demand for children in Karnataka may, on the average, be lower than in Taiwan. In 1965, desired family size in Taiwan was about 4.3 children. In the urban sector of Karnataka, desired size was already as low as 4.0 in 1951; in the rural sector it was 4.2 in 1975, but, as noted earlier, this figure is biased upward relative to those for Karnataka in 1951 and Taiwan at both dates. If family size desires in Karnataka do, in fact, tend to be lower than in Taiwan, this implies that a given increase in supply from the same initial level in the two countries would lead to an earlier growth in the motivation for control, as illustrated in figure 5.3. This is perhaps why India's transition to deliberate control has been occurring at a lower level of modernization than Taiwan's.

Differentials by Age and Socioeconomic Status

The analysis to this point has centered chiefly on trends over time, although there has been some attention to rural-urban differentials. This section points out briefly some implications of the theoretical framework for trends in fertility differentials by age and socioeconomic status and notes some supporting evidence.

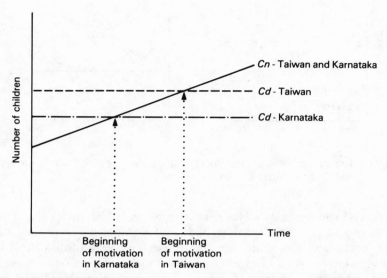

Fig. 5.3 Hypothetical Illustration of Effect of Difference in Demand for Children between Karnataka and Taiwan on Beginning of Motivation.

Age

Assume, in keeping with the model of chapters 3 and 4, that for any given couple potential supply varies with duration of marriage—the longer the marriage, the greater the potential supply, other things equal. Assume further, for simplicity, that demand and regulation costs are independent of duration of marriage. Then, if duration of marriage and age are positively correlated, one obtains the hypothetical cross-sectional patterns of supply and demand by age shown in figure 5.4. Figure 5.4A is a hypothetical sketch of how demand (*Cd*) and supply (*Cn*) might vary as the typical woman in a premodern society goes through her reproductive career. As shown, even by the end of her reproductive career, the typical woman has fewer surviving children than are desired, a situation like that of rural Karnataka in 1951. If for simplicity of exposition one disregards variations around the mean at each age, then no motivation for or adoption of fertility control exists at any reproductive age. This means that the observed age-specific marital fertility schedule in such a society would correspond to a natural fertility schedule.

Figure 5.4B is a hypothetical sketch of the same two curves later in the process of modernization. Based on the trends in tables 5.2 and

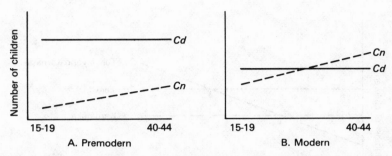

Fig. 5.4 Hypothetical Illustration of Effect on Motivation by Age of Changes in Supply and Demand during Modernization.

5.6, it is hypothesized that the *Cn* curve shifts upward and the *Cd* curve downward, as natural fertility and child survivorship improve with modernization and family size desires decline. As a result of this, a motivation to control fertility emerges at the later reproductive ages, and assuming no obstacle from regulation costs, deliberate family size limitation, occurs. With regard to the schedule of age-specific marital fertility this implies that the *trend* in age-specific fertility rates at the younger reproductive ages between situations A and B will reflect developments in natural fertility alone, and hence be upward. However, the trend at the older ages will be influenced, in addition, by a shift from uncontrolled to controlled fertility, and hence may be downward. The overall result may be a clockwise tilt in the marital fertility schedule, a development that has been noted by Knodel (1983).

In fact, the age-specific marital fertility schedules for both Karnataka and Taiwan (figs. 5.5 and 5.6) show a pattern consistent with the hypothesized developments in figure 5.4—a "tilt" upward at the younger ages, due to increased natural fertility, and downward at the older, due to the adoption of deliberate control. (The data for ages 15–19 reflect changes in age at marriage, but for the other ages this factor is negligible; see Srinivasan, Reddy, and Raju 1978, pp. 264–65, and Jejeebhoy 1979.) The absolute decline in age-specific marital fertility at older ages, despite the rise or constancy in the cumulative fertility of these age groups (tables 5.4 and 5.6) occurs because the adoption of control is concentrated at the end of the reproductive career. An implication of this analysis is that measures of period fertility, such as the general fertility rate, may increase in the early

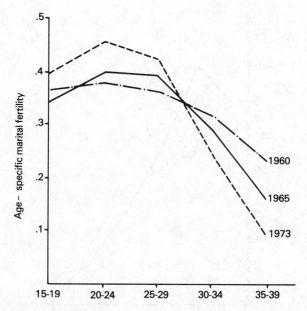

Fig. 5.5 Age-Specific Marital Fertility for the Cohort Aged 35–39 in 1960, 1965, and 1973, Taiwan. Source: Jejeebhoy 1979, p. 221.

stage of adoption of fertility control, because increased age-specific fertility at younger ages due to greater natural fertility may for awhile outweigh reduced age-specific fertility at older ages as deliberate control is adopted. This, indeed, is what happened in Karnataka (Srinivasan, Reddy, and Raju 1978, pp. 260–61).

Socioeconomic Status

Let us take years of schooling as our index of socioeconomic status. Suppose that at a given time within a country potential supply (Cn) varies positively with education (due, say, to higher natural fertility among the more educated because of shorter lactation), and demand (Cd) varies negatively, reflecting the antinatal effect of education via the taste and cost mechanisms described in chapter 2. Suppose further that the cross-sectional schedules relating supply and demand to education are positioned as shown in figure 5.7. Figure 5.7A is the premodern case; figure 5.7B, the early modern one. In Figure 5.7A

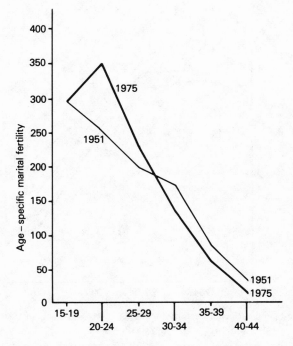

Fig. 5.6 Age-Specific Marital Fertility Rates for Bangalore, 1951 and 1975. Source: Srinivasan, Reddy, and Raju 1978, p. 252.

neither those at low nor high education levels are able to have as many children as they would like (supply, Cn, is less than demand, Cd), and, hence, those at both levels have as many as they can. In this situation, one would expect that observed fertility would vary positively with education. This appears to have been true in rural Karnataka in 1951 (table 5.8, col. 1; for Indonesia, cf. Hull and Hull 1977).

In figure 5.7B, the early modern case, the supply schedule is shifted upward and the demand schedule downward at all levels of education, as was assumed in the previous analysis of differentials by age. As a result, a motivation to control fertility occurs among those of higher education. Assuming that no obstacle arises from regulation costs, then natural fertility would prevail among lesser educated parents and controlled fertility among more educated parents. In this situation fertility differentials by education might shift from a positive to a

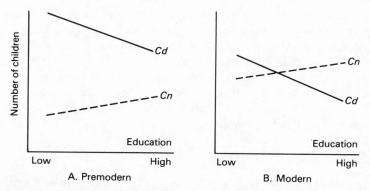

Fig. 5.7 Hypothetical Illustration of Effect on Motivation by Socioeconomic Status of Changes in Supply and Demand during Modernization.

negative slope. Again, in rural Karnataka this appears to have occurred (table 5.8, col. 2).

These results help explain the findings of Susan Cochrane (1983) in her survey of empirical studies of fertility differentials by education in developing countries. She reports a positive relation of fertility to education over part of the educational range in low income countries, and, consistent with this, that the "cross-section effect on fertility is more negative at later than at earlier points in time" (Cochrane 1983). One implication is that estimates from cross-sectional data for developing countries of the elasticity of fertility with regard to a given modernization variable such as education may yield differing results in magnitude and/or sign, depending on the relative roles of natural fertility and deliberately controlled fertility. It also implies that time series observations on national averages of, say, education and fertility

Table 5.8 General Marital Fertility Rate by Agricultural Occupation, Rural Karnataka, 1951 and 1975 (index: all rural occupations = 100)

	1951	1975
Low socioeconomic status (laborers or temporary tenants)	90	119
High socioeconomic status (other agricultural occupations)	100	96

Note: The general marital fertility rate is births per thousand continuously (1951) or currently (1975) married women aged 15–44.

Source: Srinivasan, Reddy, and Raju 1977, p. 43. One additional occupational category, "non-agricultural occupations," shown in the source is omitted here, because of uncertainty regarding its socioeconomic status ranking.

in a given country will not necessarily show the same relationship in different phases of modernization. If, for example, potential supply were rising over time as a result of decreased lactation associated with growing education but remained below demand so that natural fertility conditions persisted, then education and observed fertility would be positively associated in time. In some later period, education and fertility might be negatively associated in time as deliberate control came increasingly to prevail.

Summary and Conclusions

In this chapter, macro level survey data from the Indian state of Karnataka and the nation of Taiwan have been recast in terms of our supply-demand framework to see what light they throw on the factors causing the transition from natural fertility to deliberate fertility control. Although the data are imperfect (even after refinement to achieve as much comparability as possible), the story they tell is highly consistent and gives additional content to the theoretical view of the demographic transition presented in chapter 2 and the empirical analysis of chapters 3 and 4.

In general, it appears that in a premodern or early modern situation, the typical couple is unable to have as many surviving children as it would like even if fertility were unregulated, that is, its potential supply of children in the absence of fertility control is less than its demand for children. Because of this there is no motivation to limit fertility, and natural fertility is a rational response to the couple's basic reproductive circumstances. Also, to judge from the very limited knowledge extant about methods of fertility control, the costs of control are high; hence even those couples that are motivated to regulate fertility—those whose supply exceeds demand—may prefer to bear the burden of unwanted children rather than incur the costs of deliberate fertility regulation. For such couples also, natural fertility is a rational response to their basic reproductive circumstances.

With the progress of modernization, the typical couple shifts from a situation of deficit supply of children to excess supply. This comes about partly through a reduction in the demand for children, but more so (in the present data) through an increase in supply, due both to increased natural fertility and improved child survival. As a result, a motivation deliberately to restrict fertility emerges and grows. Also, the costs of fertility control decline as knowledge of methods of control expands. The concurrence of rising motivation for control and reduced costs of control leads to the gradual spread of deliberate fertility control throughout the population. The present data do not permit identifying the relative weights of motivation and regulation costs in promoting deliberate control, although there is a hint (in the urban-rural differentials) that motivation is more important.

The growth in deliberate family size limitation does not necessarily lead to an immediate reduction in cumulative or period fertility rates, because the fertility-enhancing effects of rising natural fertility may offset the fertility-reducing effects of deliberate regulation, which are typically concentrated among couples near the end of their reproductive careers. Both total and unwanted fertility may initially increase in conjunction with the spread of deliberate control, although the increase in each of these is less than that which would have occurred in the absence of deliberate regulation. Eventually, however, the effect of growing control prevails and both total and unwanted fertility decline.

It is possible, too, that fertility differentials by socioeconomic status may reverse during the transition to deliberate control, shifting from positive to negative (or, alternatively, becoming more negative as the transition progresses), as natural fertility conditions that initially prevailed at all socioeconomic levels are gradually replaced by deliberate fertility control occurring first among the higher socioeconomic groups. Also, the schedule of marital fertility by age is likely to show a clockwise "tilt," if adoption of control occurs first among those at older reproductive ages.

In 1975 the Indian state of Karnataka was not as far along in the shift to deliberate fertility control as Taiwan and had not yet reached the stage of declining total and unwanted fertility. However, it appears that for comparable conditions of motivation and costs of fertility control, both the adoption of control and effectiveness of control in Karnataka were as high as in Taiwan, although imperfections of the data make precise comparison difficult. But the progress of Karnataka in the shift to deliberate control has been considerably slower than that of Taiwan, probably due to its much slower pace of social and economic development. To the extent that Karnataka may be taken as indicative of India's experience more generally, there is little in this analysis to support the impression commonly encountered in the popular press that India's demographic performance has been disappointing. To judge from the present results, such impressions stem chiefly from failure to take account of the comparatively early stage of the transition in India and the fact that at this stage fertility-enhancing influences may outweigh fertility-depressing forces.

6

A Cross-Sectional Analysis of Ten Indian States

With K. Srinivasan and Shireen J. Jejeebhoy

In the last chapter survey data were used to examine in supply-demand terms the demographic transition in the Indian state of Karnataka from 1951 to 1975 and in Taiwan from 1957 to 1973. In this chapter we apply the supply-demand framework to cross-sectional data for ten Indian states in 1970. As in the previous analysis, we ask whether increased use of fertility control is associated with greater motivation, lower regulation costs, or both. This question can be asked in regard to differences among states in the use of control for both the total population of reproductive women (the first section below) and the regulating population alone (the third section). It can also be examined as regards differences within states between regulators and nonregulators (the second section).

A shortcoming of the preceding chapter was that only one measure of regulation costs was available. In the present chapter we employ a number of alternative measures embracing both attitudes toward and access to techniques of family size limitation. Also, because the analysis is conducted at the state level, we are able to include statewide indicators of family planning program services as additional measures of regulation costs. This is of special interest in providing a tentative notion of the importance of family planning programs in promoting deliberate family size limitation in India as of 1970. It thus complements the analysis of Karnataka in chapter 5, offering further insight into the factors shaping India's progress in the transition to deliberate fertility control.

Data and Methods

This analysis is based primarily on household survey data collected by the Baroda Operations Research Group (ORG) in 1970. The

148

survey, the first to aim for comprehensive coverage of family planning practices in India, was commissioned by the Ministry of Health and Family Planning, government of India, to provide information "at the national level on the current state of awareness, acceptance and adoption of family planning methods" (Operations Research Group 1971, p. 1). In the absence of a valid benchmark, evaluation of the quality of the data obtained on family planning attitudes and practices is not possible, but the survey is generally regarded by professionals as providing the best information available at the time, and it is the only one with a reasonably comprehensive geographic coverage. A common questionnaire was used in all areas, and "information was collected by fully trained interviewers through personal interviews with the respondents" (Operations Research Group 1971, p. 1).

Although the survey covered all India except for Jammu and Kashmir, North East Frontier Agency (NEFA), and the offshore islands, only data for ten states were available to us for analysis. The ten states grouped into four regions are as follows (size of sample aged 35–44 shown in parentheses):

North   Punjab, including Delhi and Haryana (576), Rajasthan (335)
Central   Madhya Pradesh (437), Uttar Pradesh (994)
West   Gujarat (372), Maharashtra (898)
South   Andhra Pradesh (585), Karnataka (481), Kerala (502), Tamil Nadu (663)

"The respondents for the survey were currently married and co-habiting women aged 15–44 years and their husbands" (Operations Research Group 1971, p. 1). In keeping with preceding chapters, only women aged 35–44 who have been married only once and have had two or more living children are included in this analysis. Half of the respondents to this survey were males who reported their wives' fertility histories and the other half were females reporting their own fertility histories. A preliminary analysis separating the female respondents and the spouses of male respondents indicated little difference between the two groups; hence they are combined so that the unit of analysis is wives. The number of wives from each state included in the analysis is given above following the state name. The mean age of these women in the various states was virtually the same.

The analysis compares the ten states, using household data compiled by the Operations Research Group, appropriately weighted for rural-urban representation, to estimate state level parameters such as

Cn, *Cd*, *s*, level of motivation, costs of regulation, and so on. We chose states as the level for analysis because of their inherent interest as social units and because family planning programs in India are primarily administered at this level (United Nations 1966, 1969). Figures for Karnataka given in this chapter differ somewhat from those in chapter 5 for several reasons: the method of estimating potential supply differs, the area surveyed differs, the age group studied differs on some measures, and the time period differs. Even with these differences, the results for Karnataka are quite consistent. Because there are only ten units of observation, the empirical analysis comprises a visual search for regular patterns in the basic data and simple correlations or, at most, multiple correlations with two independent variables, to test for significant relationships. Our interest is in identifying repetitive patterns and whether the relationships observed are consistent with those found in earlier chapters.

Most of the data for the analysis come directly from or are based on the survey. Desired family size (demand) is reported by each person interviewed. With regard to potential supply the survey data make possible an approach not feasible in the time series analysis of the preceding chapter. A proximate determinants equation is estimated by ordinary least squares from household data for each state using indicators of the proximate determinants gathered in the survey— duration of marriage, the number of years since beginning the use of fertility control, first and second surviving birth intervals, fetal wastage, infant and child mortality, and secondary sterility. Potential supply at the survey date in each state is then estimated from this equation as in chapter 3. Although the use here of ordinary least squares probably results in an underestimate of natural fertility levels in all states (Crimmins and Easterlin 1984), the directions of differences among states should be correct, and it is these that are most important for the analysis that follows. A fuller description of the estimation of potential supply is contained in the appendix to this chapter.

As mentioned, indicators of regulation costs come from both survey responses and family planning program data, the latter being available at the state level only. In the form that the indicators are presented in this chapter, costs of regulation would be expected to vary inversely with each indicator. Two dimensions of costs are measured by the survey responses: knowledge and psychological costs (or "attitudes"). As in chapters 3 and 4, knowledge is measured by the average number of contraceptive methods known by the respondents in a state and reported without special prompting. Psychological costs are indicated by responses to questions on approval of contraception and whether contraception was discussed with a spouse.

As discussed in chapters 3 and 4, in measuring the attitudinal aspect of regulation costs, one would like data that antedate the actual decision on fertility regulation, because one consequence of a decision to use control is likely to be a positive shift in the attitudes toward regulation of users relative to nonusers. For lack of such data we rely on current attitudinal data as indicative of previous attitudes, but this raises the possibility that an observed correlation between use and attitudes may reflect the effect of use on attitudes rather than vice versa. To reduce this source of bias, an analysis is also done only for users, as in the earlier chapters.

In a recent paper on measuring the impact of family planning programs, Mauldin and Lapham (1980) report a United Nations classification of program inputs into (a) funds, (b) personnel, (c) facilities, and (d) incentives. The measures of the availability of family planning services used here relate to each of these categories at an aggregative level. Additional detail for each category would also be of interest, but the comprehensive measures were readily available and seemed appropriate for an initial analysis. For the input of funds we use two measures—the cumulative total of family planning expenditures per capita, 1964–68, and per capita expenditure on medicine and public health (including family planning), 1971. Our indicators of personnel and facilities are, respectively, number of paramedical personnel per capita and primary health centers and subcenters per capita, both as of 1971. The incentive measure is the rate of payment per client for vasectomy in 1965. The three 1971 measures refer to health rather than family planning programs alone, and postdate the fertility control decisions we seek to explain which were mostly taken in the 1960s. In most states, however, health and family planning programs tended to expand together, and the state differences as of 1971 typically reflected the buildup of these programs over the years.

The dependent variable, use of fertility control, is measured from the survey data in two ways: (1) by the percentage of respondents reporting that they have ever used one of the following methods of fertility control—vasectomy, tubectomy, IUD, pill, condom, diaphragm, jelly, foam tablets, coitus interruptus, rhythm, abstinence, or lactation (as a method of fertility control); (2) by the number of years since respondents began the use of fertility control. (Induced abortion as a technique of fertility control was not covered in the survey.) Years since use began is determined from responses to questions on children's ages and the number of births before first use. The number of years since a woman began contraception is assumed to be equal to the age of the surviving child whose order corresponds to the birth after which use began. This underestimates the duration of contraceptive use for women who have experienced child mortality. On the other hand, as previously discussed, it is likely to overestimate length of use, because it makes no allowance for lapses from use. Despite these shortcomings, we believe the measure is a reasonable indicator of differences among states in the extent of use of deliberate family size limitation. In keeping with this measure of fertility control and the nature of the sample, the concept of fertility employed throughout is the cumulative number of live births per married woman at the survey date.

Results

Variations among States: Total Population

In the ten Indian states covered here, about 28 percent of females aged 35–44 report practicing contraception at some time in their reproductive careers, from a low of 13 percent in Uttar Pradesh to 42 percent in the Punjab (table 6.1). The length of use, as reflected in mean years since starting use, is low, averaging only 2.3 years, and ranging from one year in Uttar Pradesh to 3.8 in the Punjab. However, when the length-of-use measure is confined to users alone, the average rises to 8.0 years, differences among states are narrowed, and the ranking is altered somewhat. In the present section we focus on mean years since starting use for all women, not just regulators alone, and states in table 6.1 and subsequent tables are ranked by this measure. This is the best single indicator of state differences in the extent of use, reflecting both the proportion using and the length of use among those regulating their fertility. The results would be virtually identical, however, if the percentage ever using were taken as the dependent variable; the correlation coefficient between this and years since first use is .99. In the third section of this chapter we analyze differences among states in the length of use for regulators alone.

An indicator used in the Indian family planning program of the cumulative performance of the program up to March 1971 is also shown in table 6.1. Cumulative performance is measured as the prevalence of contraception among couples at risk. Specifically, this denotes

Table 6.1 Percent Ever Using Fertility Regulation, and Mean Years Since Starting Fertility Control, 1970, and Cumulative Performance of Family Planning Program up to March 1971, Selected Indian States

| State | Percent ever using fertility regulation | Mean years since starting contraceptive use | | Cumulative performance (Prevalence of contraception among couples at risk, 1971) |
		All women	Women who have used fertility regulation	
Punjab	42.4	3.79	9.76	18.3
Maharashtra	41.1	3.26	7.77	18.2
Tamil Nadu	39.1	3.26	8.63	15.8
Gujarat	34.1	3.08	9.23	15.5
Kerala	35.7	2.83	8.27	16.6
Andhra Pradesh	23.8	1.63	6.85	13.2
Karnataka	17.5	1.34	7.73	9.4
Rajasthan	19.0	1.30	6.90	5.4
Madhya Pradesh	15.4	1.03	6.74	10.5
Uttar Pradesh	12.8	1.02	8.24	6.0
Unweighted average	28.1	2.25	7.97	12.9

Source: Unless otherwise specified, data in this and subsequent tables are from the survey reported in Operations Research Group 1971. Col. 4 is from Srinivasan et al. 1972.

the percent of couples of reproductive age effectively protected up to March 1971, taking into account discontinuation of method, mortality of either spouse during the wife's reproductive period, and exit of wife from the reproductive ages. Although the ranking by states according to this measure does not fit perfectly the ranking created from the measures gathered from the ORG survey, the correlation coefficients between the survey measures and the measure of cumulative perform- ance are quite high (.92 with percentage ever using and .90 with years since starting fertility regulation). This suggests that our analysis may throw light on the factors responsible for state differences in family planning program performance.

Our analysis here of demand, supply, and regulation costs follows the lines of previous chapters. With regard to supply, we estimate the average output in 1970 for women in these states as 4.7 children in the absence of deliberate fertility control, with a range from around 4.3 in

154   Chapter 6

Madhya Pradesh and Uttar Pradesh to 5.1 in the Punjab and Kerala (table 6.2, col. 3). Note that these orders of magnitude are similar to those estimated in the preceding chapter for Karnataka—around 4.3 in 1951 and 5.4 in 1975 (compare table 5.1). As has repeatedly been observed, variations in supply (in this case, among states) reflect contributions by both natural fertility and child survivorship—the correlation coefficient between Cn and N is .63, between Cn and s, .78 (cf. also cols. 1, 2, and 3 of table 6.2).

The demand for children in these states is somewhat less than supply, averaging about 4.2 children. Across states, demand typically varies inversely with supply (the correlation coefficient is $-.84$), the high being 4.8 children in Uttar Pradesh and the low, 3.6 in the Punjab (col. 4). Again, these magnitudes are similar to those for Karnataka in the preceding chapter (table 5.2). In three states (Rajasthan, Madhya Pradesh, and Uttar Pradesh) supply is somewhat short of demand, on the average, and in one (Andhra Pradesh) it only slightly exceeds demand (col. 5). Thus, in four of ten states covered here, there was, on the average, little or no motivation for control as late as 1970, a situation similar to that found in the preceding chapter for rural Karnataka in 1951. This adds further support to the view advanced there that the typical situation in a premodern or early modern society is one where couples have difficulty in achieving their desired family size even under the best of circumstances. In the other six states the average situation is one of positive motivation, the excess of supply

Table 6.2 Mean Values of Natural Fertility (N), Proportion of Children Surviving (s), Supply (Cn), Demand (Cd), and Motivation (Cn-Cd), Selected Indian States, 1970

State	N	s	Cn	Cd	Cn-Cd
Punjab	6.40	.797	5.10	3.56	1.54
Maharashtra	5.86	.817	4.79	3.96	.83
Tamil Nadu	6.18	.777	4.80	3.88	.92
Gujarat	6.19	.800	4.95	4.12	.82
Kerala	5.96	.864	5.15	3.95	1.20
Andhra Pradesh	5.86	.763	4.47	4.27	.21
Karnataka	6.05	.813	4.92	4.01	.91
Rajasthan	6.06	.746	4.52	4.63	$-.11$
Madhya Pradesh	5.47	.779	4.26	4.44	$-.18$
Uttar Pradesh	6.04	.720	4.35	4.75	$-.40$
Unweighted average	6.01	.788	4.73	4.16	.58

over demand ranging from about 0.8 children in Maharashtra and Gujarat to 1.5 in the Punjab. Differences among states in motivation are due about equally to supply and demand, the correlation coefficients of Cn and Cd with $Cn - Cd$ are respectively, .95 and $-.96$.

In the preceding chapter we found that in the rural area of Karnataka the measure of motivation increased from $-.35$ in 1951 to 1.05 in 1975 (table 5.2). This range brackets the average values for all but three states in table 6.2. Although we do not have data available to test the idea, we conjecture that motivation has been increasing over time in all of these states and that, like Karnataka, many of the states may have shifted only recently into a situation of excess supply of children.

As previously mentioned, states in table 6.2 are ordered according to their average length of use of fertility control, as indexed by years since first use. Visual inspection of the table shows that states with high use typically have a higher supply of children, lower demand, and higher motivation. Simple correlation confirms that these relationships are significant (table 6.3, line 1). Use is not significantly related to number of surviving children, C, but it is to the actual number of unwanted children, $C - Cd$. As shall be seen, however, $C - Cd$ performs relatively poorly in the multivariate analysis for the total population below and also in the subsequent analysis of the regulating population.

Allowing for the small number of units of observation here, the patterns among Indian states so far observed are consistent with those of the preceding chapters. In general, supply and demand are inversely related and both contribute to motivating fertility control. Use of

Table 6.3 Correlation Coefficient between State Mean of Years Since First Use of Fertility Regulation and Specified Measure of Motivation

Variable	Measure of motivation				
	Cn-Cd	C-Cd	C	Cd	Cn
Years since first use of fertility regulation	.85*	.78*	.53	$-.84*$	.77*
Cn-Cd (potential unwanted children)	—	.99*	.82*	$-.96*$	.95*
C-Cd (actual unwanted children)		—	.88*	$-.94*$	.96*
C (surviving children)			—	$-.66*$	.93*
Cd (demand)				—	$-.84*$
Cn (supply)					—

*Significant at .05 level or better. Sample size = 10.

control is directly related to the level of motivation, and, of the alternative motivation measures considered, none is superior and typically they are inferior. To this point, the analysis tends to support the view that differences among Indian states in the use of fertility control are at least partly due to differences in the underlying reproductive supply and demand conditions.

We turn next to regulation costs. State indicators of the costs of regulation available from the ORG survey (measures of approval, spousal communication, and knowledge) are given in table 6.4. As previously discussed, these ex post measures suffer from the problem that causation can run from use to the measure of regulation costs as well as vice versa. Specifically, with regard to approval a couple may practice contraception without approving of it, and if, say, no ill effects arise from the use of contraception, then change to approval. Similarly, causation in the spousal communication measure can run in both directions—spouses who communicate better about family planning are more likely to use it, but those who use family planning are more likely to discuss it with their spouses. An analogous bias in number of methods known was pointed out in chapter 3.

This problem of possible bias does not afflict the state-level mea-

Table 6.4 Percent Approving of Contraception and Discussing Contraception with Spouse, and Mean Number of Contraceptive Methods Known (unprobed), Selected Indian States, 1970

| | Percent of respondents | | |
| | --- | --- | --- |
State	Approving of contraceptive use	Discussing family planning with spouse	Mean number of contraceptive methods known (unprobed)
Punjab	63.8	33.2	1.79
Maharashtra	62.4	29.3	1.79
Tamil Nadu	55.3	29.1	1.76
Gujarat	54.8	28.9	1.86
Kerala	59.0	37.8	2.13
Andhra Pradesh	48.4	29.6	1.51
Karnataka	38.8	19.0	.77
Rajasthan	30.0	12.9	1.17
Madhya Pradesh	27.4	13.9	.75
Uttar Pradesh	27.0	20.1	1.01
Unweighted average	46.7	25.4	1.45

sures of family planning program inputs—facilities, personnel, expenditures, and incentive payments (table 6.5). For this reason, they are somewhat better indicators of state differences in regulation costs. As noted, these measures are also of interest for testing the effectiveness of family planning programs in promoting deliberate fertility control. In general, since family planning program activities tend to legitimate use of control, increase knowledge of techniques of control, and provide family planning services at below market cost, they lower the cost of fertility control—thus regulation costs would vary inversely with the availability of program services.

Altogether, we have eight indicators of regulation costs—three based on the ORG survey and five relating to family planning. Examining the relationships among them, one finds that the survey-based

Table 6.5 Family Planning Program Indicators for Selected Indian States, Specified Dates

State	(1) Primary health centers, 1971	(2) Para-medical personnel, 1971	(3) Expenditure on medicine and public health, 1971–72	(4) Incentive payments, 1965	(5) Family planning expenditure, 1964–68
Punjab	6.33	148.2	7.24	10	1.32
Maharashtra	6.28	76.8	7.49	10	1.29
Tamil Nadu	8.25	88.2	8.29	30	1.21
Gujarat	6.75	25.4	7.01	15	1.49
Kerala	8.23	37.1	7.17	17	1.69
Andhra Pradesh	3.83	40.8	6.32	10	.89
Karnataka	7.63	33.8	5.07	15	.97
Rajasthan	4.84	21.7	8.84	0	.89
Madhya Pradesh	6.83	26.4	4.89	0	.84
Uttar Pradesh	4.79	13.8	3.10	10	.69
Unweighted average	6.38	51.2	6.54	12	1.13

Sources: Col. 1, number of centers and subcenters per 100,000 population, 1971, from Government of India 1976, table 36. Col. 2, number of personnel (nurses, auxiliary nurse midwives, midwives, health visitors) registered up to 1971 per 100,000 population, from Government of India, 1976, tables 51, 52. Col. 3, per capita expenditure (rupees) on medicine and public health during 1971–72, from Government of India 1976, table 64. Col. 4, financial assistance (rupees) per client for male sterilization, 1965, from United Nations 1966, p. 66. Col. 5, cumulative family planning expenditure per capita, 1964–68, from United Nations 1969, p. 14.

measures are quite closely related, the lowest correlation coefficient between any two being .89 (table 6.6). In contrast, none of the family planning variables is significantly correlated to any other, although all of them are positively correlated. The lack of any significant associations among the family planning measures is somewhat puzzling. It may mean simply that the measures capture different and independent dimensions of the program. But it may signify that some of these measures are seriously flawed as indicators of family planning program activity. In any event, the fact that there are five family planning measures not significantly correlated with each other would seem to increase the likelihood that at least one of these measures would show a significant relation to use of control, and, to the extent the measures do capture different program dimensions, perhaps indicate which aspect is more effective in promoting use.

Examination of the relationships between the ORG survey and family planning measures shows that, in general, 1964–68 family planning expenditure and 1971 paramedical personnel are the family planning measures most closely related to the survey-based measures of costs of regulation. All of the measures—including both survey and family planning measures—are positively correlated, though some only weakly.

To what extent do these indicators of regulation costs show an association with use of fertility control? From inspection of table 6.4, where states are ordered according to contraceptive use, one can see that the ORG survey measures are related to use in the expected direction, and table 6.6 confirms that these relationships are significant with correlations ranging between .80 and .94. Thus, use of control is positively associated with more favorable attitudes, better spousal communication, and knowledge of more methods. However, as one might expect, the picture is more mixed for the family planning measures. Only two of the five indicators, 1971 availability of paramedical personnel and 1964–68 family planning expenditures, are significantly positively related to contraceptive use.

So far, then, our simple correlations suggest that both motivation and regulation costs are associated in the expected way with use of fertility control, although a few measures fail to show significant relationships. What measures hold up best in multivariate analysis? To answer this, first order partial correlations were computed between years since first use and each measure of motivation in table 6.3, controlling successively for each cost measure in table 6.6, and, then,

Table 6.6 Correlation Coefficient between State Mean of Years Since First Use of Fertility Regulation and Specified Measure of Costs of Regulation

Variable	Costs of regulation							
	Percent approving	Percent discussing with spouse	Number of methods known	Primary health centers	Paramedical personnel	Expenditures on medicine and public health	Incentive payments	Family planning expenditure
Years since first use of fertility regulation	.94*	.80*	.87*	.44	.76*	.60	.54	.82*
Percent approving	—	.90*	.89*	.37	.70*	.55	.54	.83*
Percent discussing with spouse		—	.90*	.30	.52	.32	.59	.80*
Number of methods known			—	.26	.47	.61	.50	.86*
Primary health centers				—	.22	.19	.60	.61
Paramedical personnel					—	.41	.30	.37
Expenditures on medicine and public health						—	.21	.53
Incentive payments							—	.48

*Significant at .05 level or better. Sample size = 10.

between use and each regulation cost measure, controlling for each motivation measure.

With regard to the motivation measures, $Cn - Cd$ and one of its components, Cd, perform best. For example, when $Cn - Cd$ is put in competition with the various regulation cost measures, it is significant and the regulation cost measure, not significant in five cases—spousal communication, primary health centers, paramedical personnel, health expenditures, and incentive payments (compare table 6, 7, line 1 of panels A and B). Both $Cn - Cd$ and the regulation cost measure are significant when $Cn - Cd$ is coupled with number of methods known, and neither is significant when $Cn - Cd$ is paired with family planning expenditure, 1964–68. In only one case is $Cn - Cd$ not significant and the regulation cost measure, significant; this is when $Cn - Cd$ is put up against approval of family planning. The only difference between the performance of Cd and that of $Cn - Cd$ is in the pairing with family planning expenditure—in the case of $Cn - Cd$, neither the motivation nor cost measure is significant; in the case of Cd, both are significant.

Examining the performance of the regulation cost measures against the two best motivation measures, $Cn - Cd$ and Cd, the only cost measure that comes out clearly better is approval of family planning (neither motivation measure is significant in the pairing with approval, while approval is significant in both pairings). Number of methods known and family planning expenditure are next best, holding their own against the two motivation measures. Note, however, that two of the three cost measures that fare best are suspect for possible bias, approval and number of methods known. Among the five bias-free family planning measures only one is not dominated by the motivation measures, and this one, family planning expenditure, only holds its own.

To make sure that these results were not attributable to the choice of years since first use as the dependent variable, multiple correlations were also run replacing the dependent variable, years since first use, first with the ever used measure of table 6.1 (col. 1) and then with the contraceptive prevalence measure (col. 4). The results were virtually the same as those reported here for years since first use.

The multivariate analysis thus helps us further to weed out more from less promising measures of motivation and regulation costs. On the motivation side, the theoretically preferred measure of motivation, $Cn - Cd$, appears best, along with one of its components, Cd, the demand for children. On the side of regulation costs, approval of

Table 6.7 First Order Partial Correlation between Years Since First Use of Fertility Regulation and Specified Measure of Motivation or Costs of Regulation

Measure of Motivation		Measure of costs of regulation						
	Percent approving	Percent talking with spouse	Number of methods known	Primary health centers	Paramedical personnel	Expenditure on medicine and public health	Incentive payments	Family planning expenditure
A. Partial correlation with specified motivation measure, controlling for specified regulation cost measure								
Cn-Cd (potential unwanted children)	.13	.61*	.71*	.81*	.67*	.81*	.78*	.53
C-Cd (actual unwanted children)	-.06	.47	.58	.61*	.71*	.68*	.31	-.06
C (surviving children)	-.20	.10	.12	.37	.59*	.41	.37	-.41
Cd (demand)	-.12	-.64*	-.79*	-.81*	-.59*	-.81*	-.78*	-.64*
Cn (supply)	.10	.47	.49	.71*	.69*	.70*	.68*	.20
B. Partial correlation with specified regulation cost measure, controlling for specified motivation measure								
Cn-Cd (potential unwanted children)	.78*	.45	.75*	-.20	.44	.46	.13	.43
C-Cd (actual unwanted children)	.85*	.54	.76*	-.13	.58*	.44	.20	.51
C (surviving children)	.92*	.71*	.81*	.18	.79*	.51	.39	.79
Cd (demand)	.78*	.51	.82*	-.12	.25	.48	.18	.58*
Cn (supply)	.85*	.55	.73*	-.06	.68*	.44	.23	.48

*Significant at .05 level or better. Sample size = 10.

family planning methods performs best, followed by number of methods known and family planning expenditure, which both perform about equally well. Allowing for possible bias in the survey-based cost measures, however, the results remain ambiguous as to which are the best cost and motivation measures, and the relative strengths of each. The analysis for the regulating population in section 3 should help reduce this ambiguity. First, however, we turn briefly to intrastate comparisons of the regulating and nonregulating populations as another test of the framework.

Variation within States: Regulating and Nonregulating Populations

Based on the theoretical model, we expect that in each state, on average, the motivation level of regulators, as measured by the excess of supply over demand, should exceed that of nonregulators, and/or the fertility control costs of regulators should be lower than those of nonregulators. To investigate this, table 6.8 presents for regulators

Table 6.8 Mean Values of Supply (Cn), Demand (Cd), and Motivation ($Cn\text{-}Cd$) for Users and Nonusers of Contraception, Selected Indian States

State	Cn			Cd			$Cn\text{-}Cd$		
	Users	Non-users	U-NU	Users	Non-users	U-NU	Users	Non-users	U-NU
Punjab	5.65	4.69	.96	3.43	3.64	−.21	2.22	1.04	1.18
Maharashtra	5.20	4.49	.71	3.86	4.03	−.17	1.34	.47	.87
Tamil Nadu	5.39	4.43	.96	4.14	3.71	.43	1.25	.71	.54
Gujarat	5.51	4.65	.86	3.72	4.32	−.60	1.81	.32	1.49
Kerala	5.38	5.02	.36	3.81	4.03	−.22	1.57	.99	.58
Andhra Pradesh	5.08	4.29	.79	4.02	4.34	−.32	1.05	−.06	1.11
Karnataka	5.82	4.72	1.10	4.04	4.01	.03	1.79	.72	1.07
Rajasthan	5.12	4.38	.74	3.60	4.87	−1.27	1.53	−.48	2.01
Madhya Pradesh	4.94	4.13	.81	4.24	4.47	−.23	.71	−.34	1.05
Uttar Pradesh	5.26	4.19	1.07	3.87	4.87	−1.00	1.39	−.62	2.01
Unweighted average	5.34	4.50	.84	3.87	4.23	−.36	1.47	.28	1.19

and nonregulators separately the mean values in each state of demand, supply, and the difference between them, motivation. As expected, the motivation to regulate fertility is uniformly higher among regulators than among nonregulators: by less than one child in Maharashtra, Tamil Nadu, and Kerala; by between 1.0 and 1.2 children in Punjab, Andhra Pradesh, Karnataka, and Madhya Pradesh; and by between 1.5 and 2.0 children in Gujarat, Rajasthan, and uttar Pradesh (col. 9).

Examining the contributions to differences in motivation of differences in supply and demand, one finds that supply is the more important factor. In every state regulators have a greater potential supply of children than nonregulators and in all but two states they have a lower demand, but the numerical contribution of the supply difference to motivation is always greater than that of demand, with the sole exception of Rajasthan (compare col. 3, 6, and 9). Thus, the lower motivation observed among nonregulators as compared with regulators is due more to a lower potential supply than to a higher demand, although both usually contribute. Data not presented indicate that the lower supply of nonregulators is, as usual, due to both lower natural fertility and lower child survival.

The regulation cost indicators that are available separately for regulators and nonregulators are confined to the three ORG survey measures—approval, spousal communication, and number of methods known. Table 6.9 shows, as hypothesized, that by every one of these measures users of fertility control have lower regulation costs than nonusers. However, this difference could reflect the effect of use, rather than vice versa.

Data presented earlier in tables 4.5 and 4.6 enable us to make similar comparisons of regulators and nonregulators within Sri Lanka and Colombia. As for the Indian states, we consistently observe that regulators (U) have a higher supply, lower demand, and higher motivation than nonregulators (NU):

	Cn			Cd			Cn − Cd		
	U	NU	U − NU	U	NU	U − NU	U	NU	U − NU
Sri Lanka	6.7	5.9	0.8	4.4	5.0	−0.6	2.4	1.0	1.4
Colombia	8.0	6.8	1.2	4.5	5.6	−1.1	3.5	1.2	2.3

Again, supply contributes more than demand to the difference between the two groups in motivation, although the supply-demand differences here are small. With regard to regulation costs, the differences between regulators and nonregulators are again like those in the Indian states, with regulators consistently showing lower costs:

	Number of methods known			Proximity to nearest family planning outlet					
				Distance, km.			Travel time, min.		
	U	NU	U – NU	U	NU	U – NU	U	NU	U – NU
Sri Lanka	2.6	1.4	1.2	—	—	—	—	—	—
Colombia	5.1	2.8	2.3	3.4	5.6	−2.2	23.7	44.1	−20.4

Note that for Colombia this turns out to be true of the family planning measures of proximity to outlets, with users reporting closer proximity. Unfortunately, these family planning measures cannot be assumed to be bias-free, because the effect of use may be to improve knowledge of proximity to outlets and thus cause the observed difference in responses of users and nonusers.

Table 6.9 Percent Approving of Contraception and Discussing Contraception with Spouse and Mean Number of Contraceptive Methods Known (unprobed) for Users and Nonusers of Contraception, Selected Indian States

	Percent of respondents								
	Approving of contraceptive use			Discussing family planning with spouse			Mean number of contraceptive methods known		
State	Users	Non-users	U-NU	Users	Non-users	U-NU	Users	Non-users	U-NU
Punjab	89.6	44.3	45.3	66.8	8.5	58.3	3.07	.91	2.16
Maharashtra	87.3	44.2	43.1	55.2	11.2	44.0	2.57	1.25	1.32
Tamil Nadu	71.8	44.7	27.1	47.4	17.3	30.1	2.55	1.25	1.30
Gujarat	88.4	36.6	51.8	55.0	15.4	39.6	2.89	1.33	1.56
Kerala	81.5	46.4	35.1	72.4	18.6	53.8	2.64	1.86	.78
Andhra Pradesh	85.5	36.2	49.3	83.7	12.7	71.0	2.72	1.13	1.59
Karnataka	85.0	28.4	56.6	71.5	7.8	63.7	1.93	.74	1.19
Rajasthan	78.1	18.3	59.8	56.9	2.5	54.4	2.74	.80	1.94
Madhya Pradesh	75.3	19.0	56.3	61.6	5.2	56.4	2.12	.50	1.62
Uttar Pradesh	87.2	17.3	69.9	74.2	12.2	62.0	3.05	.68	2.37
Unweighted average	83.0	33.5	49.4	64.5	11.1	53.3	2.63	1.04	1.58

In sum, the results of the intrastate analysis are consistent with those from our earlier analysis of Sri Lanka and Colombia and also with the simple correlations in the preceding section. Both a higher level of motivation and lower regulation costs (as reflected in the survey measures) are associated with the practice of fertility control. However, the cost measures in this section are confined to those subject to possible bias.

Variation among States: Regulating Population

The dependent variable of this section, years since first use of fertility control for the regulating population, is shown in table 6.1, column 3. In general, one would expect that states in which the regulating population started controlling its fertility earlier would, other things equal, show higher levels of motivation among regulators. Table 6.10 presents for the regulating population the simple correlations of use with the various motivation measures and also the correlations among the motivation measures themselves (the underlying data for the motivation measures are in tables 6.8 and 6.13). As expected, the supply-demand measure of motivation, $Cn - Cd$, is significantly positively related to years since first use. The two components of this measure, supply (Cn) and demand (Cd), both show the expected direction of relationship, but unlike the findings for the total population, only supply is significant. Neither the number of living children (C) nor unwanted children ($C - Cd$) is significantly related to use. Comparing these results with those for the total population (table 6.3),

Table 6.10 Correlation Coefficient between State Mean of Years Since First Use of Fertility Regulation and Specified Measure of Motivation, Regulating Population

Variable	Measure of motivation				
	Cn-Cd	C-Cd	C	Cd	Cn
Years since first use of fertility regulation	.72*	.19	−.38	−.47	.69*
Cn-Cd	—	.80*	.03	−.79*	.83*
C-Cd (unwanted children)		—	.38	−.73*	.59
C (surviving children)			—	.35	.37
Cd (demand)				—	−.32
Cn (supply)					—

*Significant at .05 level or better. Sample size = 10.

one finds that, in general, the theoretically preferred measure, $Cn - Cd$, most consistently shows a significant positive association with use.

As noted, separate indicators of regulation costs for users of fertility control are available only for the ORG survey measures (see table 6.9). It seems reasonable to suppose, however, that the statewide family planning differences shown in table 6.5 would apply to the regulating as well as the total population in each state—in other words, that regulators in states with more active family planning programs would have lower costs of control by virtue of these programs than regulators in states with less active programs. On this assumption we include the family planning measures of table 6.5 along with the ORG survey measures of table 6.9 in examining the relation of use to costs of control for the regulating population alone.

For the ORG survey measures the correlations for the regulating population are strikingly different from those for the total—now, none of the ORG survey measures are significantly associated with use (table 6.11, cols. 1–3). Thus, within the regulating population there is no consistent association between years since starting control and the favorableness of attitudes, spousal communication, or number of methods known. This suggests that the significant correlations for the total population between use and the ORG survey measures (table 6.6) are due to the effect of use, rather than vice versa, a result similar to that found for individual households in Sri Lanka and Colombia in chapter 4 (cf. table 4.5). As regards the correlations of the family planning program measures with use, the results are also poorer than those for the total population—now only one of the measures, 1964–68 family planning expenditure, shows a significant simple correlation with use, and it is at the dividing line for significance (.62).

For the regulating population, then, simple correlation reveals significant associations between use and two measures of motivation— the theoretically preferred measure, $Cn - Cd$, and one of its components, Cn—and between use and only one indicator of regulation costs, family planning expenditure. Turning to partial correlation, table 6.12 replicates for the regulating population the analysis of table 6.7 for the total population—each motivation measure of table 6.10 is paired with each cost measure of table 6.11 as independent variables and the partial correlations with use computed. The results point to the importance of the preferred measure of motivation, $Cn - Cd$, in determining use of fertility control. The partial correlation of use with $Cn - Cd$ is significant in every one of the eight pairings of $Cn - Cd$ with

Table 6.11 Correlation Coefficient between State Mean of Years Since First Use of Fertility Regulation and Specified Measure of Costs of Regulation, Regulating Population

Variable	Percent approving	Percent discussing with spouse	Number of methods known	Primary health centers	Paramedical personnel	Expenditures on medicine and public health	Incentive payments	Family planning expenditure
Years since first use of fertility regulation	.38	−.26	.50	.43	.51	.13	.59	.62*
Percent approving	—	.44	.45	−.36	.15	−.27	−.15	.16
Percent discussing with spouse		—	.06	−.44	−.22	−.56	−.22	−.27
Number of methods known			—	−.45	.26	.16	.01	.18

*Significant at .05 level or better. Sample size = 10.

Table 6.12 First Order Partial Correlation between State Mean of Years Since First Use of Fertility Regulation and Specified Measure of Motivation or Costs of Regulation, Regulating Population

Measure of Motivation	Percent approving	Percent discussing with spouse	Number of methods known	Primary health centers	Paramedical personnel	Expenditure on medicine and public health	Incentive payments	Family planning expenditure
							Measure of costs of regulation	
A. Partial correlation with specified motivation measure, controlling for specified regulation cost measure								
Cn-Cd (potential unwanted children)	.66*	.74*	.66*	.72*	.64*	.71*	.76*	.62*
C-Cd (actual unwanted children)	-.01	.29	.11	.27	.08	.16	.34	.08
C (surviving children)	-.40	-.31	-.05	-.49	-.34	-.37	-.54	-.33
Cd (demand)	-.34	-.48	-.19	-.65*	-.35	-.46	-.76*	-.34
Cn (supply)	.63*	.72*	.82*	.61*	.63*	.69*	.56	.61*
B. Partial correlation with specified regulation cost measure, controlling for specified motivation measure								
Cn-Cd (potential unwanted children)	-.06	-.36	.35	.43	.06	-.05	.66*	.47
C-Cd (actual unwanted children)	.16	-.34	.49	.46	.49	.09	.64*	.61*
C (surviving children)	.39	-.11	.36	.52	.49	.08	.68*	.60*
Cd (demand)	.16	-.29	.27	.62*	.41	-.06	.80*	.55
Cn (supply)	.16	-.37	.72*	.14	.38	.17	.39	.52

*Significant at .05 level or better. Sample size = 10.

regulation costs (panel A, line 1). No other motivation measure does as well, although Cn does almost as well. Conversely, when the relationship between use and each cost variable is considered, controlling for $Cn - Cd$, the partial correlations are all insignificant, with one exception (panel B, line 1). Surprisingly, the exception is not family planning expenditure, the cost measure that showed a significant simple correlation with use; family planning expenditure, when put in competition with $Cn - Cd$ in multiple correlation, drops to insignificance. Rather the exception is incentive payments, which is significant along with, but not instead of, $Cn - Cd$. For the total population, however, the incentive measure was not significantly associated with use either in the simple correlation or in a partial correlation when paired with $Cn - Cd$ (tables 6.6 and 6.7, panel B).

Throughout the analysis, then, the measure that shows up most consistently in explaining use is $Cn - Cd$. By comparison, the alternative motivation measures and the indicators of regulation costs— whether the subjective survey-based measures or family planning indicators—perform, at best, erratically. As a whole, these results point to the importance of the excess of supply over demand in determining the use of contraception. This finding is consistent with those of chapter 4, although there the family planning measure for Colombia (proximity to outlets) did consistently show a significant, though weak, association with use (see tables 4.8 and 4.9).

Fertility Control and Fertility

In itself, greater use would imply lower fertility; but since states with greater use also tend to have higher natural fertility, the relation of use and actual fertility is not evident a priori. Chapter 5 showed that as use spreads within a population over time, it may initially be accompanied by constant or even increasing natural fertility. Not until possibly 50 percent or more of married women aged 35–44 are controlling fertility does observed fertility decline (table 5.6). In the present data only two states exceed even 40 percent use; if the earlier findings are pertinent, then one might expect to find little evidence here of a negative association between use and actual fertility.

As a basis for testing this, table 6.13 presents data on both the number of children ever born and the number of surviving children for the total, regulating, and nonregulating population in each state. As in previous tables, the states are listed in order of decreasing extent of use. A glance at columns 1 and 2 for the total population confirms our

Table 6.13 Average Number of Children Ever Born (B) and Surviving Children (C) for Total, Regulating, and Nonregulating Population, Selected Indian States, 1970

State	Total		Regulators		Nonregulators	
	B	C	B	C	B	C
Punjab	5.94	4.75	5.51	4.71	6.26	4.78
Maharashtra	5.57	4.55	5.62	4.72	5.54	4.44
Tamil Nadu	5.89	4.59	6.04	4.77	5.80	4.46
Gujarat	6.04	4.84	5.76	4.66	6.18	4.93
Kerala	5.85	5.06	5.49	4.83	6.04	5.17
Andhra Pradesh	5.87	4.48	6.38	4.97	5.71	4.33
Karnataka	5.99	4.89	6.26	5.27	5.93	4.81
Rajasthan	5.91	4.51	6.32	4.80	5.82	4.45
Madhya Pradesh	5.49	4.28	6.11	4.77	5.38	4.19
Uttar Pradesh	5.94	4.26	5.68	4.66	5.97	4.17
Unweighted average	5.85	4.62	5.92	4.82	5.86	4.57

expectations—there is little evidence of a systematic difference in fertility or surviving children associated with increasing use. The correlation coefficient with years since first use is .11 for fertility and .53 for surviving children, neither of which is significant.

Within states, regulators have higher fertility than nonregulators in six of ten cases, and more surviving children in seven of ten cases, a result again consistent with the fact that one is observing populations in an early stage of the transition to deliberate control (cols. 3–6). However, when one compares states with regard to the fertility of regulators alone, there is a significant negative association with use, suggesting that the negative impact of use on actual fertility is starting to dominate. Number of surviving children, however, is not significantly correlated with use.

Thus, as suggested in chapter 5, the comparative level of actual fertility is not itself a good indicator of the stage of the transition to deliberate fertility control. Some Indian states are considerably further advanced with regard to the motivation for fertility control and these states show more response in the actual use of control; their levels of fertility, however, are not significantly less than in states with little use of control.

Summary and Conclusions

The main concern of this chapter was to explain differences among ten Indian states in the use of fertility control, as reported in a special 1970 survey conducted by the Baroda Operations Research Group. In keeping with the theoretical framework, we hypothesized that such differences might arise from differences in the motivation for fertility control and/or differences in regulation costs. As possible indicators of motivation, we examined our theoretically preferred measure, the excess of supply over demand $(Cn - Cd)$, and its individual components; also, the actual number of surviving children (C) and the actual number of unwanted children $(C - Cd)$. With regard to regulation costs, in addition to our usual measure of family planning knowledge, number of methods known, attitudinal data were available for the first time on the favorableness of attitudes toward family planning and whether spouses talked with each other about family planning. In addition, with states as the unit of analysis, it was possible to include measures of family planning program inputs as indicators of regulation costs, and thus to test whether family planning programs had a significant independent impact in promoting fertility control.

Our results suggest that the chief reason that the use of fertility control was more advanced in 1970 in some Indian states than others was that motivation, in the sense of the excess of the supply of children over demand, was higher in the states with greater use. As in chapter 4, the theoretically preferred measure of motivation performed better in the empirical analysis than alternative measures such as the actual number of unwanted children $(C - Cd)$ and number of surviving children (C). Taken separately, the components of the preferred measure Cn and Cd, sometimes performed as well as (though not better than) $Cn - Cd$, but not consistently so. Thus, the theoretically preferred measure was also the best measure empirically. Again, this is consistent with the results of chapter 4.

Higher levels of fertility control may also arise from perceived costs of regulation that are below average. Our data do indicate that in states with greater use of control attitudes toward family planning are more favorable, spousal communication is greater, and knowledge of methods is better. However, use may affect attitudes and knowledge, as well as vice versa, and when we correct for this bias by confining our analysis to the regulating population alone, we no longer obtain significant associations between use and attitudes, spousal communication, or knowledge.

Five family planning program indicators were used here—two measues of expenditures and one each of personnel, facilities, and incentive payments. Of these, only one—1964–68 family planning program expenditure—was significantly associated with use of control in bivariate correlations for both the total and regulating populations, and this dropped to insignificance when paired with $Cn - Cd$ in partial correlation analyses. Incentive payments, along with $Cn - Cd$, was significantly associated with use in a multiple correlation for the regulating population. For the total population, however, the incentive measure was not significant in a multiple correlation, while $Cn - Cd$ was; nor was it significant in a simple bivariate correlation with use. Thus, after trying five family planning measures, none of which is significantly correlated with any other, we find no consistent evidence of an impact of the family planning program on use of control independent of motivation.

This result suggests some caution in inferences about state differences in the performance of family planning programs. As we have seen, the Indian program measure used in evaluating performance is positively correlated with the principal dependent variable analyzed here, years since first use of contraception. Our results imply that state differences in this measure of family planning program performance are attributable to differences in population motivation, not to differences in family planning program inputs.

The family planning program measures used here are, of course, imperfect, and this may account for their poor performance. In chapter 4, we saw that in Colombia a somewhat different family planning program indicator, proximity to outlets, performed significantly, though weakly when motivation ($Cn - Cd$) was controlled (tables 4.8 and 4.9). However, chapter 5 did suggest a substantive reason why the present results may be valid—that resources in the Indian family planning program may have been misallocated in targeting them for the less motivated rural rather than urban population.

Regulation costs aside, the results of this chapter generally show a pattern like that observed in chapters 4 and 5: (1) use of control is positively associated with motivation, $Cn - Cd$, (2) motivation reflects the influence both of supply and demand, and (3) supply differences stem from both natural fertility and child survival. Also, little association was found between state differences in the use of control and those in actual fertility. This conforms to the expectation based on the analysis of chapter 5 that in the early stages of the transition from natural to controlled fertility, observed fertility may be constant or even rising as the positive effect on observed fertility of higher natural fertility offsets the negative effect of greater control.

Appendix: Method of Estimating Natural Fertility and Potential Supply

Natural fertility at the household level is estimated by a proximate determinants analysis that is a variant of the approach used by the authors in chapters 3 and 4. For households within each of the ten states of India the number of living children is regressed on indicators of the underlying proximate determinants including years of use of fertility control. The resulting equations (shown in table 6A.1) are then used to estimate for each household the number of living children that would exist if fertility control had never been used by the couple. This is done by taking the relevant state equation and substituting back into the equation the household values for each of the independent variables except the years of use of fertility control, which is set equal to zero for each household. The estimate of potential living children is then converted to an estimate of potential children ever born by using the child survival rate actually experienced by the individual couple. Mean values for each state are obtained by averaging the household estimates.

The independent variables on which the number of living children is regressed include duration of marriage, the interval from marriage to the birth of the first surviving child, the interval between the births of the first and second surviving children, an indicator of secondary sterility, the percent of pregnancies ending in fetal death, the percent of live-born children who have died, and the number of years since the birth of the living child corresponding to the parity at which the use of contraception began.

The variables employed were sometimes chosen because of data availability rather than perfect correspondence with those theoretically desirable. For instance, because only the ages of living children were reported in the survey, the more desirable birth interval mea-

174

Table 6A.1 State Regression Equation for Estimate of C_n (standard error in parentheses)

State	Second birth interval (months)	First birth interval (months)	Infant and child mortality ratio	Duration of marriage (years)	Not secondarily sterile (0/1)	Proportion of pregnancy wastage	Years since first use[a]	Constant	R^2
Punjab	−.0206* (.0025)	−.0159* (.0018)	−1.4028* (.3313)	.2090* (.0136)	2.2996* (.1534)	−1.0045* (.4873)	−.1029* (.0091)	.5165	.4257
Maharashtra	−.0220* (.0017)	−.0171* (.0014)	−1.7495* (.2522)	.2128* (.0099)	2.0238* (.1107)	−.7408 (.4698)	−.0930* (.0082)	.6928	.4681
Tamil Nadu	−.0250* (.0021)	−.0194* (.0018)	−1.6175* (.2972)	.2166* (.0127)	2.1909* (.1435)	−1.1021* (.4466)	−.0502* (.0097)	.6425	.4692
Gujarat	−.0213* (.0030)	−.0180* (.0019)	−1.4813* (.3955)	.1995* (.0152)	2.2172* (.1902)	−.8836 (.6313)	−.1052* (.0122)	.8486	.4409
Kerala	−.0295* (.0026)	−.0219* (.0022)	−1.8496* (.3715)	.2775* (.0128)	2.2658* (.1525)	−.8041 (.6002)	−.0581* (.0104)	−.3225	.5790
Andhra Pradesh	−.0189* (.0020)	−.0199* (.0015)	−1.9210* (.2775)	.1939* (.0119)	2.1694* (.1289)	−1.5004* (.6219)	−.0419* (.0136)	.8404	.4863
Karnataka	−.0233* (.0025)	−.0185* (.0019)	−1.9476* (.3475)	.2256* (.0145)	2.4098* (.1417)	−1.7820* (.7376)	−.0773* (.0158)	.4381	.5426
Rajasthan	−.0244* (.0028)	−.0226* (.0022)	−1.7583* (.3624)	.1932* (.0164)	2.0236* (.1849)	−1.3470* (.6533)	−.0621* (.0172)	1.4847	.5064
Madhya Pradesh	−.0183* (.0024)	−.0156* (.0017)	−1.7285* (.3286)	.1486* (.0140)	1.7429* (.1634)	−1.8688* (.6296)	−.0461* (.0169)	1.8577	.3922
Uttar Pradesh	−.0215* (.0014)	−.0190* (.0011)	−2.0462* (.1917)	.1923* (.0092)	1.9769* (.1048)	−1.0979* (.4141)	−.0740* (.0011)	1.3289	.5004

*Significant at .05 level or better.
Note: Sample size: see text, section on data and methods.
[a]Set to zero for estimating C_n.

sures based on the history of all births rather than surviving ones could not be employed. The use of these surviving birth interval measures also explains why surviving children rather than children ever born is used as the dependent variable in the regression.

Secondary sterility was inferred from data on the use of contraception and the length of the open birth interval. Among women who have never contracepted, those with an open surviving birth interval of less than seven years are classified as fecund; those with an open birth interval of seven years or longer are considered secondarily sterile. Among women who have ever contracepted, those currently contracepting and past contraceptors whose open surviving birth interval is less than ten years are considered fecund. The use of ten rather than seven years is based on the assumption that among those who ever used who are not current users, past use may have averted fertility for about three years. Past users whose open surviving birth interval is ten years or greater are assumed to be secondarily sterile. All currently pregnant women no matter what the length of their birth interval are classified as fecund.

IV
Conclusion

7
Summary and Implications

Social and economic modernization has everywhere been accompanied by a fertility revolution—the spread of deliberate family size limitation within marriage and a decline in childbearing from levels averaging around six or more births per woman over the reproductive career to around two. The reasons for this fertility revolution are the central problem of this volume. In seeking answers, a supply-demand theory of fertility determination is tested and applied to data for various developing areas.

The Theory

The key issue on which the theory focuses is the causes of adoption of deliberate fertility control. The word "deliberate" should be emphasized. Childbearing in a premodern society is often characterized as "natural" or uncontrolled fertility. But "uncontrolled" in this context means only the absence of deliberate intent by parents to limit family size. There may be various living conditions or other circumstances that keep childbearing below the biological maximum. Amenorrhea associated with prolonged breastfeeding, for example, is known frequently to have an important effect on family size, but the dominant motivation for breastfeeding is the concern of parents for the health and wellbeing of their child, not family size as such. The most important issue in explaining the fertility revolution is what causes parents deliberately to adopt techniques that limit fertility within marital or consensual unions.

In sociology the answer to this question is usually sought in terms of the concepts of "motivation," "attitudes," and "access." Parents are more likely deliberately to regulate their fertility, it is reasoned, if

179

(1) they are more highly motivated, (2) they have more favorable subjective attitudes toward techniques of fertility control, and (3) they have easier access to such techniques, that is, to obtaining knowledge of methods, to purchasing contraceptive supplies and services, and so on.

The framework adopted here formalizes these sociological notions in terms of an economic theory of childbearing. Motivation is seen as a matter of a couple's reproductive supply and demand conditions; hence the shorthand designation, a supply-demand theory (although supply and demand are defined differently here than in microeconomic theory). Attitudes and access are grouped together under the rubric costs of fertility regulation. The reasoning is this: As regards motivation, a couple forms a notion of the number of surviving offspring it would produce if it did nothing deliberately to limit its fertility. This notion of "potential supply" is based on various clues from the couple's reproductive career. For example, in developing countries relatively few couples limit their fertility prior to the second birth, if at all; hence the pace of early childbearing provides one indication of their potential fertility. This potential supply is weighed against their demand for children, approximated here by desired family size. If supply falls short of demand, there is no motivation to regulate fertility and their childbearing will be uncontrolled, that is, they will exhibit natural fertility, in the sense described above. If potential supply exceeds demand, parents will be motivated to limit their fertility to avoid a loss in well-being due to unwanted children—the greater the excess of supply over demand, the greater this motivation. This concept of motivation, it should be noted, differs from the usual one in demographic analysis, which is confined to the demand for children alone.

Even if there is motivation, however, deliberate restriction of fertility does not necessarily take place. This is because the use of techniques of fertility control entails various costs—such as subjective drawbacks associated with distaste for the use of various methods (e.g., abstinence or withdrawal) or actual costs in time and money involved in the use of some techniques (e.g., abortion, sterilization, or the contraceptive pill). The decision on adopting fertility control involves weighing the costs associated with its use against the motivation to do so (or, put differently, against the costs of unwanted children arising from failure to use). Adoption is more likely the greater a couple's potential supply, the lower its demand, and the less its perceived costs of fertility regulation. The theory thus focuses attention on these three variables—demand, supply, and regulation costs—as the key to the fertility control decision. Changes associated with modernization—agricultural innovation, industrialization, urbanization, compulsory public schooling, public health measures, and so on—are seen as affecting this decision via their impact on one or more of these three variables.

Empirical Results

This theory raises a number of straightforward empirical questions. Is it true, in fact, that greater use of fertility control is found to go with greater motivation, that is, with a larger excess of the potential supply of children over the demand for children? Does more use of control occur when the perceived costs of regulating fertility are lower? If both motivation and regulation costs are linked in the expected way to use of fertility control, which has the greater influence? What is the immediate stimulus to increased motivation—variations in the demand for children, supply, or both? Is the low use of fertility control in a premodern demographic situation due to lack of motivation to control fertility or high regulation costs (i.e., unfavorable attitudes toward or limited access to methods of family size limitation)? Is the transition to deliberate family size limitation a result of growing motivation, declining regulation costs, or both? How is adoption of control linked to the actual rate of childbearing, and what are the trends in actual fertility, births averted, and unwanted children as family size limitation spreads in a society?

To answer these and related questions, several bodies of data are analyzed—household (micro) data for Sri Lanka and Colombia from the mid-1970s, aggregative population (macro) data for the Indian state of Karnataka and the nation of Taiwan spanning two decades up to the mid-1970s, and macro data for ten states of India around 1970. The population analyzed is women close to the end of their reproductive career (those aged 35–44) who have been continuously married and (except in chapter 5) have had at least two children. The results of these studies, reported in chapters 3 through 6, are very consistent. We first summarize the specific results for motivation and regulation costs and then discuss the sequential pattern of the causes of the fertility revolution. Finally, we note some implications for research, policy, and the world population problem.

Motivation for Fertility Control

The concept of motivation for fertility control and its empirical implementation are perhaps the most important innovations in the present approach. How do they stand up to the data? The answer is, remarkably well. In both micro and macro data and, as regards the latter, both time series and cross-sectional data, we find that the motivation for fertility control as measured here, that is, the excess of the supply of over the demand for children, is consistently and significantly related to use of control both in simple correlation and multiple regression analysis (see, for example, tables 4.8, 4.9, 5.3, 5.6, 6.7, and 6.12). Moreover, this measure of motivation performs better than several alternatives commonly used in the literature—whether respondents want more children, how many living children they already have, how many they desire, and length of marriage (Tables 4.5, 6.7, and 6.12). It seems unlikely that these results could be a statistical artifact. They do not depend on any single measure of or technique of estimating the supply of children, the component of motivation most difficult to estimate. Although we devise our own (micro) approach to estimating supply in chapter 3, it is compared with alternatives (chap. 4, appendix) and different approaches are used in the macro analyses of chapters 5 and 6 as dictated by the available data. We conclude that the varied evidence examined here supports the hypothesis that those households that envisage unregulated fertility as leading to a family size considerably in excess of that desired are under greater pressure to use deliberate control.

How important is the demand for children in determining the motivation for fertility control—is high motivation, for example, principally a matter of low family size desires? Or is supply also important? Our results indicate that both supply and demand contribute to motivation, and, in the phase of the fertility transition covered by our data, supply is as important as demand and possibly more important. This is a major finding, because motivation for fertility control is commonly identified with demand alone. The importance of supply is underscored by table 7.1, which draws on data from the earlier chapters plus Nepal, a country of special interest because of its very low use of deliberate control. The striking feature of the table is the wide variation in use of control among the various geographic areas, despite quite similar family size desires (demand). The principal explanation of this apparent anomaly is the large differences among the areas in the potential supply of children. This results in substantial differences in

Table 7.1 Use of Fertility Control, Demand for Children, Supply of Children, and
Motivation for Fertility Control, Continuously Married Women Aged 35–44
with Two or More Children, Four Countries in the 1970s

Country and year	(1) Average years since first use	(2) Percent ever using	(3) Demand for children Cd	(4) Supply of children Cn	(5) Motivation for fertility control, Cn-Cd
Colombia, 1976	7.3	69	4.8	7.6	2.8
Sri Lanka, 1975	4.3	56	4.6	6.4	1.7
India, 1970	2.3	28	4.2	4.7	0.6
Nepal, 1976	0.4	8	4.4	4.3	−0.1

Source: Sri Lanka and Colombia, tables 4.5 and 4A.1; India (unweighted average of ten
states), tables 6.1 and 6.2; Nepal (Amatya, forthcoming). Data for India are for women
with two surviving children rather than two live births and are based on a somewhat
different technique for estimating supply that biases the estimate somewhat downward
(appendix to chap. 6 and chap. 4).

motivation that largely account for the observed variation in use of
control. As for the reasons for variations in potential supply, the
analyses in this volume suggest that, in general, natural fertility and
child survival are both contributing factors, but that neither one uniformly dominates.

Regulation Costs

The measure of costs of fertility control used most frequently in this
study was a respondent's unprompted knowledge of methods of limiting fertility, the idea being that those more acquainted with varied
techniques of family size limitation are in a better position to choose a
method that they perceive as less costly. Hence regulation costs vary
inversely with number of methods known. Although this measure is
the one most widely available in the data, in some data sets it was
possible to try a number of other cost measures. Hence, at times we
also used measures of attitudes toward fertility control, such as per-
missible reasons for abortion, approval of family planning, and the
extent to which spouses discuss fertility control, and measures of
access to fertility control, such as time of travel and distance to family
planning services, and the supply of family planning services, as mea-

sured by number of establishments, number of paramedical personnel, and family planning expenditures.

In simple correlations, we obtained results like those common in
the literature: these measures almost always showed the expected
associations with use of control—the lower the costs, the greater the
use (tables 4.6, 5.3, 5.6, 6.6, 6.11). But for some measures the cause-
effect interpretation of this result is complicated by the fact that use
itself tends to lower regulation costs, by promoting more favorable
attitudes, better knowledge of methods, and so on. This problem is
less serious if nonusers are eliminated from the analysis. But when this
was done, the correlations of these cost measures with use were usually
no longer significant (table 4.6, panel B; table 6.11). An important
exception was proximity to family planning outlets in Colombia. This
had a low but significant association with use in the expected direction
for both the total and regulating populations even after controlling for
motivation. In contrast, various aggregative measures of family planning inputs in India did not perform well, but there may be substantive
reasons for this. For one thing, the Indian family planning program
targeted the less motivated segment of the population, that living in
rural areas. Also, the program promoted almost exclusively a "ter-
minal" method, vasectomy, which is likely to be perceived by many
potential clients as having high regulation costs, both because it involves an operation and because it is irreversible.

Thus, in general, we find an indication that regulation costs as
indexed by proximity to family planning services, has the expected
relation to use, but the picture is more ambiguous for other measures.
It is possible that this is because of defects in our regulation cost
measures and that further work with data that provide better and more
comprehensive measures would alter this conclusion. This is doubtless
an important issue for further research. However, for the present
measures, and times and places covered in this study, the conclusion to
which our results uniformly point is the dominant importance of
motivation, as conceptualized here, in the adoption and use of fertility
control (tables 4.8, 4.9, 6.7, and 6.12).

The Causes of the Fertility Revolution

This volume started by posing the question of the causes of the
fertility revolution. In only one chapter (5) are changes over time
actually studied, but the patterns found there are quite consistent with
the results of the cross-sectional analyses in the other chapters. The

general picture that emerges of the early phase of the transition to deliberate fertility control—up to, say, 50 percent use among married women aged 35–44—is this. In a premodern situation there is little use of control because couples typically cannot have as many children as they desire. Observed fertility is, in consequence, natural or uncontrolled fertility—uncontrolled in the sense that parents do not attempt deliberately to restrict their fertility, though fertility may be unintentionally limited by physiological conditions or by breastfeeding or other behavioral patterns motivated predominantly by concerns other than family size. With the onset of modernization, the number of children that would result from unregulated fertility gradually comes to exceed desired family size, and an incentive to limit family size emerges and grows. The growing excess of the potential supply of children over demand seems to be especially due to increases in parents' potential supply, though usually declining demand also contributes. This conclusion raises some doubts about the notion that a decrease in desired family size must precede adoption of deliberate fertility control, because increasing supply alone might push families into adoption. A rise in supply is typically due both to declining infant and child mortality and increasing natural fertility, the latter possibly due to a shortening or abandonment of breastfeeding. Also, as modernization progresses, the costs of fertility control trend downward, and this, too, would tend to induce greater adoption. However, we found only limited evidence of an independent effect of regulation costs on use of control, once motivation was taken into account.

In this early stage of the transition, there may be little or no change in observed fertility—indeed, an increase in fertility is even possible—because the fertility-lowering effect of greater use of control tends to be offset by rising natural fertility. Moreover, the measured trend in unwanted children may be upward; the effect of fertility control in averting births is largely to forestall an even greater rise in unwanted children.

Initially fertility control is probably used only for short periods and not very efficiently. However, associated with the spread of control there is a growth in both the length and efficiency of use, and eventually, the spread of control translates into fertility decline, though perhaps not until after use has spread to 50 percent of married women aged 35–44.

These generalizations, it should be recalled, are based on empirical studies relating primarily to the early phase of the fertility transition in a few areas. It is quite possible that the relative weights of different factors, such as supply versus demand or motivation versus regulation costs, may vary during the transition or be different elsewhere.

Research Implications

Recent work on the fertility transition has underscored the variability in the experience of different countries. As Knodel and van de Walle (1979) observe: "The most striking finding to emerge from the recent upsurge of research on the fertility transition in Europe is that it occurred under remarkably diverse socioeconomic and demographic conditions"; in particular, "there was no clear threshold of social and economic development required for the fertility transition to begin" (pp. 220, 225). The present analysis makes clear why this may be so. As shown in figure 5.3, the effect of any given modernization factor, such as public health, varies depending on the initial conditions of (and, implicitly, changes in) other modernizing and cultural variables. Because of this, there is no necessity for any one aspect of modernization, or even some selected set of modernization variables, to exhibit an invariant pattern in relation to observed fertility and the adoption of fertility control. Indeed, the surprising thing is that mortality and fertility change were ever sufficiently closely related in historical experience to suggest the well-known model of the demographic transition. The most reasonable expectation is of considerable variability in the association between fertility decline and individual aspects of modernization. Although in all countries that have modernized or are modernizing there are a number of similar changes in social, economic, and political conditions, their relative timing has by no means been uniform. Also, economic changes, such as shifts in industrial structure, are often protracted, whereas social changes, such as those in public health or compulsory elementary education, may be more concentrated temporally. Moreover, in today's developing countries advances in public health and compulsory education often occur at an earlier time relative to economic modernization than was true of the now-developed countries, and in these countries new modernizing influences are at work, such as mass media in the form of radio, television, and movies, new modes of fertility regulation such as the pill and IUD, and government population programs sometimes of a coercive nature. Cultural conditions, too, vary widely, both within and between the more and less developed blocs. Hence the ways in which various modernizing and cultural influences come together to shape demand, supply, and regulation costs, and, thus, the fertility revolution, should not be expected to be identical from one place to another.

Most of the empirical analysis in this volume has been on links from demand, supply, and regulation costs to fertility and fertility control. Chapter 4 did present some tentative findings on links from modernization to demand, supply, and regulation costs, but the possibilities open to exploration were constrained by the data available (tables 4.11–4.18). In our view the most important next step in implementing empirically the supply-demand approach is in clarifying the specific channels through which modernization impinges on the three central variables of the framework.

Our analysis also touched on differentials in fertility within a society by socioeconomic status (SES). Chapter 5 showed that the trend in fertility differentials by SES may vary systematically during modernization, depending particularly on whether natural fertility, deliberately controlled fertility, or a mix of the two predominates. The theoretical analysis in that chapter indicated, for example, that the negative relation often presumed to hold between fertility and level of education is not necessarily typical of countries in a premodern situation or at an early stage of the fertility transition and that fertility differentials by education may shift from positive to negative as the transition occurs (or, alternatively, become more negative). This result helps explain the varied findings of Susan Cochrane (1983) in her survey of empirical studies of fertility differentials by education in developing countries.

To turn to another aspect of fertility differentials, several studies reported by John Knodel (1983) show a "tilt" in the age-specific marital fertility schedule with the progress of modernization—an increase at younger ages and a decrease at older. This development is linked by Knodel to the predominance of natural fertility behavior at younger ages and deliberate family size limitation at older. Chapter 5 presents additional evidence of this phenomenon and shows, in terms of the present theory, how the mechanisms generating the emergence of the motivation for fertility control tend to have a differential impact by age that may produce the observed tilt in the age-specific marital fertility schedule.

As Knodel also points out, the net balance of these contrasting fertility changes at younger and older ages or, alternatively, of natural versus deliberately controlled fertility at various ages may yield a stable or even upward movement in the total fertility rate at an early stage in the shift to deliberate fertility control. It is important to recognize this when one seeks to assess the state of the fertility transition in a particular country. In the Indian family planning program, for example, fertility targets were repeatedly set on the assumption that increased fertility control went hand-in-hand with declining fertility, and the failure to achieve the fertility targets led some observers to discount India's progress (Nortman 1978 provides an excellent survey). As we have seen in chapters 5 and 6, however, stable or even increasing fertility is possible in the early phase of the adoption of deliberate fertility control. The comparison of Karnataka with Taiwan in chapter 5 suggests that India has not lagged in the adoption of fertility control, when proper allowance is made for the comparative state of motivation and regulation costs. This analysis also demonstrates how the present theoretical framework can be used to structure comparative study of the adoption of fertility control in different societies.

As noted in chapter 2, a number of current theories of the demographic transition tend to emphasize only one, or at most two, of the three central variables in our analysis—demand, supply, and regulation costs—with most stress being placed either on conditions working to lower the demand for children or to reduce regulation costs. Our empirical findings suggest that the emphasis of such theories may be somewhat misplaced, at least as regards the phase of the transition to deliberate control studied here. Of the three factors, changes in the supply of and demand for children that increase motivation appear most important in generating adoption of control, with changes in regulation costs, seemingly less significant. Also, as between supply and demand, supply is as important as demand, and possibly more important. These are, of course, empirical results and could be overturned by further work—the theory itself is neutral as regards the relative weight of the three factors. These results do, however, suggest the need for reconsideration of current theories of the demographic transition and particularly the desirability of incorporating systematically the supply of children and its underlying determinants.

Policy Implications

The theoretical analysis of chapter 2 noted a number of ways in which modernization processes and, by implication, modernization policies might affect the variables of demand, supply, and regulation costs, and, through these, fertility and fertility control. For the present purpose we distinguish several broad policy areas: (1) economic development policies, such as agricultural modernization, industrial development, and international trade policies; (2) social modernization programs, such as universal compulsory schooling, public health, and maternal and child health programs; and (3) family planning policies. In terms of our framework, it seems likely that the main impact of the first two program areas is via the supply and demand variables and, through these, on the motivation for fertility control; of the third policy area, family planning, on costs of regulating fertility. For example, agricultural modernization, industrialization, compulsory schooling, and public health programs tend to lower the demand for children and increase the supply, with the net result of raising the motivation for fertility control (table 2.1). In contrast, family planning programs operate chiefly on access to fertility control by providing below cost family planning services. Also, they may promote favorable attitudes toward deliberate family size limitation by providing social legitimation for the use of contraceptive methods that might otherwise be viewed as alien to one's culture. In both respects, family planning programs lower regulation costs.

This tying of socioeconomic development policies to motivation and family planning to regulation costs is, of course, an oversimplification. For example, the modernizing effect of new institutions like the school or factory may make individuals more receptive to adoption of new techniques like family planning (in our terminology, may lower regulation costs, cf. Inkeles and Smith 1974). Correspondingly, family planning policies that promote the small family ideal operate on motivation by lowering demand. But these are not the main ways in which such programs are usually thought to work.

Consider now the implications of the analysis for several issues that arise in deciding on policies to lower fertility in a developing country:

1. How should funds be allocated between socioeconomic development policies, on the one hand, and family planning programs, on the other?

2. What segments of the population should be targeted for family planning programs?

3. What methods of family planning should be promoted?

To one impressed by the problem of persistent high fertility and unaware of the factors responsible for it, the answers to these questions might well be: push family planning programs, target the highest fertility segment of the population, and stress irreversible methods—what might be called, in total, the "high fertility" policy package.

In contrast, the present analysis suggests the following: First, the optimum policy mix between socioeconomic development and family planning programs depends on the stage of modernization. Early in the modernization process, when motivation is low or lacking altogether, socioeconomic development policies should take precedence; only as positive motivation emerges and grows does family planning warrant a growing share of resources. Second, the targeting of populations (e.g., in different geographic areas or socioeconomic groups) for family planning should be based on their motivation for fertility control, that is, the extent of the excess of their potential supply over demand. High fertility is not itself a reliable guide. If, for example, it is coupled with especially low child survival, as might be true among low-income segments of the population, or a very high demand for children, the subject population may not yet be as motivated for fertility control as other segments of the population with lower fertility. And third, methods should be promoted that are perceived by the target populations as entailing low regulation costs. Irreversible methods and/or those requiring surgical procedures may be viewed as having serious drawbacks and thus may be less readily adopted by many of those motivated for fertility control.

In practice, the emphasis over the last two decades has often leaned more toward the "high fertility" policy package than that suggested by the present study. If our analysis is correct, the limited success of the "high fertility" package is due to premature emphasis on family planning policies and misdirection of resources in such programs in terms of target populations and techniques promoted. Family planning programs have a legitimate role to play in promoting fertility control, but they need to be formulated with proper attention to the population's state of motivation and perceived costs of regulation.

The Population Problem

A word, finally, on implications of the present study for the future. To some, the post–World War II population explosion in developing countries is the world's most urgent problem, and drastic measures are needed to stem the high rates of population growth that have emerged. The analysis here leads to a more moderate view.

The source of the present high growth rates of population is the sharp reduction in mortality accomplished largely by the spread of public health programs in the Third World—itself a welcome development. Although some analysts see rapid rates of population growth as a serious obstacle to economic development, the fact is that since

World War II living levels in the Third World have generally improved, often at rates higher than ever before. In this respect, today's Third World countries are replicating the historical experience of the now-developed countries, where accelerating population and per capita income growth went together, though today's rates of change—both economic and demographic—are typically higher (Easterlin 1968, Kuznets 1966, Morawetz 1977).

Projection of the present high rates of population growth for another century or so leads quickly to a despairing view of the world's future. The validity of such projections, however, turns on the likelihood of persistent high fertility in the Third World. In this regard, the lesson of the present analysis is that the process of socioeconomic modernization that lies behind the present increased growth rates both of population and per capita income is also operating to bring about fertility reduction. By raising the supply of children and lowering demand, socioeconomic modernization is pushing the populations of developing countries into a situation of increasing motivation for fertility control. At the same time it is lowering regulation costs by undermining cultural barriers to the adoption of fertility control and increasing the availability of contraceptives, often in conjunction with family planning programs. Thus pressures for family size limitation are mounting as obstacles to use of fertility control diminish. True, too little is known yet about the specific links between modernization and the fertility revolution, but it appears that the more rapid the process of modernization, the more rapid the transition to lower fertility. Thus, this analysis of the causes of the fertility revolution leads to a view of the population explosion as a transient phenomenon.

Bibliography

Amatya, Ramesh. Forthcoming. "Comparative Analysis of the Transition to Deliberate Fertility Control and Its Links to Modernization in Seven Asian Nations." Ph.D. diss., University of Southern California.

Becker, Gary S. 1960. "An Economic Analysis of Fertility." In Universities-National Bureau Committee for Economic Research (ed.), *Demographic and Economic Change in Developed Countries*, 209–31. Princeton: Princeton University Press.

———. 1965. "A Theory of the Allocation of Time." *Economic Journal* 75 (September): 493–517.

Berk, Richard A. 1983. "An Introduction to Sample Selection Bias in Sociological Data." *American Sociological Review* 48 (June): 386–98.

Bongaarts, John. 1978. "A Framework for Analyzing the Proximate Determinants of Fertility." *Population and Development Review* 4:105–32.

———.1982. "The Fertility-Inhibiting Effects of the Intermediate Fertility Variables." *Studies in Family Planning* 13(6):179–89.

———. 1983. "The Proximate Determinants of Natural Marital Fertility." In R. Bulatao and R. D. Lee, eds., *Determinants of Fertility in Developing Countries: A Summary of Knowledge*. New York: Academic Press.

Bongaarts, John, and Jane Menken. 1983. "The Supply of Children: A Critical Essay." In R. Bulatao and R. D. Lee, eds., *Determinants of Fertility in Developing Countries: A Summary of Knowledge*. New York: Academic Press.

Bourgeois-Pichat, Jean. 1967a. "Relation between Foetal-Infant Mortality and Fertility." *Proceedings of the World Population Conference, 1965* 2:68–72. New York: United Nations.

———. 1967b. "Social and Biological Determinants of Human Fertility in Nonindustrial Societies." *Proceedings of the American Philosophical Society* 3(3) (June): 160–63.

Bulatao, Rodolfo A., and Ronald D. Lee, eds. 1983. *Determinants of Fertility in Developing Countries: A Summary of Knowledge*. New York: Academic Press.

Bumpass, Larry A., and Charles F. Westoff. 1970. "The 'Perfect Contraceptive' Population." *Science* 169 (September 18): 1177–82.

Caldwell, John C. 1983. "Direct Economic Costs and Benefits of Children." In R. Bulatao and R. D. Lee, eds., *Determinants of Fertility in Developing Countries: A Summary of Knowledge.* New York: Academic Press.

Caldwell, John C., and P. Caldwell. 1977. "The Role of Marital Sexual Abstinence in Determining Fertility: A Study of the Yoruba in Nigeria." *Population Studies* 31:193–217.

Caldwell, John C., P. H. Reddy, and P. Caldwell. 1983. "The Causes of Marriage Change in South India." *Population Studies* 37(3) (November): 343–61.

Carlsson, Gosta. 1966. "The Decline of Fertility: Innovation or Adjustment Process?" *Population Studies* 20(2) (November): 149–74.

Chang, Ming-Cheng. 1978. "Migration and Fertility in Taiwan." Ph.D. diss., University of Pennsylvania.

Chen, S. 1963. "Pattern of Fertility in Taiwan: Report of a Survey Made in 1957." *Journal of Social Science* 13:209–94.

Coale, Ansley J. 1975. "The Demographic Transition." *The Population Debate: Dimensions and Perspectives* 1:347–55. New York: United Nations.

Coale, Ansley J., and T. James Trussell. 1974. "Model Fertility Schedules: Variations in the Age Structure of Childbearing in Human Populations." *Population Index* 40 (2) (April): 185–258.

———. 1975a. "A New Method of Estimating Standard Fertility Measures from Incomplete Data." *Population Index* 41:182–210.

———. 1975b. "Erratum." *Population Index* 41:572–73.

Cochrane, Susan H. 1979. *Fertility and Education: What Do We Really Know?* World Bank Staff Occasional Papers, no. 26. Baltimore: Johns Hopkins University Press.

———. 1983. "Effects of Education and Urbanization on Fertility." In R. Bulatao and R. D. Lee, eds., *Determinants of Fertility in Developing Countries: A Summary of Knowledge.* New York: Academic Press.

Coleman, J. S. 1968. "Modernization, II—Political Aspects." In David L. Sills, ed., *International Encyclopedia of the Social Sciences* 10:395–402. New York: Macmillan.

Crimmins, Eileen M., and Richard A. Easterlin. 1984. "The Estimation of Natural Fertility: A Micro Approach." *Social Biology* 31 (Summer). Forthcoming.

Davis, Kingsley, and Judith Blake. 1956. "Social Structure and Fertility." *Economic Development and Cultural Change* 4 (3) (April): 211–35.

Easterlin, Richard A. 1968. "Economic Growth: An Overview." In David L. Sills, ed., *International Encyclopedia of the Social Sciences* 4:395–408. New York: Macmillan.

———. 1970 "An Approach to Fertility Analysis for LDC's." Paper prepared for June 29–July 3, 1970, meeting of the United Nations Ad Hoc Commit-

tee of Experts on Programs in Demographic Aspects of Economic Development. New York: United Nations.

————. 1975. "An Economic Framework for Fertility Analysis." *Studies in
Family Planning* 6 (March): 54–63.

————. 1978. "The Economics and Sociology of Fertility: A Synthesis." In
C. Tilly, ed., *Historical Studies of Changing Fertility*. Princeton: Princeton
University Press.

Easterlin, Richard A., and Eileen M. Crimmins. 1982. "An Exploratory Study
of the 'Synthesis Framework' of Fertility Determination with World Fertility Survey Data." *Scientific Reports* 40 (November). Voorburg, Nether-
lands: International Statistical Institute.

Easterlin, Richard A., Robert A. Pollak, and Michael L. Wachter. 1980.
"Toward a More General Economic Model of Fertility Determination:
Endogenous Preferences and Natural Fertility." In Richard A. Easterlin,
ed., *Population and Economic Change in Developing Countries*. Chicago:
University of Chicago Press.

Freedman, Ronald. 1975. *The Sociology of Human Fertility*. New York: John
Wiley.

Government of India. 1976. *Health Statistics of India, 1971 to 1975*. New
Delhi: Government of India Press.

Gray, Ronald. 1983. "The Impact of Health and Nutrition on Natural Fertil-
ity." In R. Bulatao and R. D. Lee, eds., *Determinants of Fertility in
Developing Countries: A Summary of Knowledge*. New York: Academic
Press.

Harris, Marvin. 1968. *The Rise of Anthropological Theory*. New York:
Thomas Y. Crowell.

Hermalin, Albert I. 1983. "Fertility Regulation and Its Costs: A Critical
Essay." In R. Bulatao and R. D. Lee, eds., *Determinants of Fertility in
Developing Countries: A Summary of Knowledge*. New York: Academic
Press.

Hull, Terence H., and Valerie J. Hull. 1977. "The Relation of Economic Class
and Fertility: An Analysis of Some Indonesian Data." *Population Studies*
31 (1): 43–57.

Inkeles, Alex. 1969. "Making Men Modern: On the Causes and Consequences
of Individual Change in Six Developing Countries." *American Journal of
Sociology* 75 (2) (September): 208–25.

Inkeles, Alex, and David H. Smith. 1974. *Becoming Modern*. Cambridge,
Mass.: Harvard University Press.

Jain, A. K., and J. Bongaarts. 1981. "Socio-Biological Factors in Exposure to
Childbearing: Breastfeeding and Its Fertility Effects." *World Fertility Survey Conference, 1980: Record of Proceedings* 2:255. Voorburg, Nether-
lands: International Statistical Institute.

Jejeebhoy, Shireen J. 1978. "The Transition from Natural to Controlled
Fertility in Taiwan: A Cross-Sectional Analysis of Demand and Supply
Factors." *Studies in Family Planning* 9(8): 206–11.

————. 1979. "The Transition from Natural to Controlled Fertility in Taiwan." Ph.D. diss., University of Pennsylvania.

————. 1981. "Cohort Consistency in Family Size Preference." *Studies in Family Planning* 12:229–32.

Kirk, Dudley. 1971. "A New Demographic Transition." In National Academy of Sciences, *Rapid Population Growth*, 123–47. Baltimore: Johns Hopkins University Press.

Knodel, John. 1977. "Family Limitation and the Fertility Transition: Evidence from the Age Patterns of Fertility in Europe and Asia." *Population Studies* 31 (July): 219–49.

————. 1983. "Natural Fertility: Age Patterns, Levels, Trends." In R. Bulatao and R. D. Lee, eds., *Determinants of Fertility in Developing Countries: A Summary of Knowledge*. New York: Academic Press.

Knodel, John, and V. Prachuabmoh. 1973. "Desired Family Size in Thailand: Are the Responses Meaningful?" *Demography* 10:619–38.

Knodel, John, and Etienne van de Walle. 1979. "Lessons from the Past: Policy Implications of Historical Fertility Studies." *Population and Development Review* 5(2) (June): 217–45.

Knodel, John, Napaporn Havanon, and Anthony Pramualratana. 1983. "A Tale of Two Generations: A Qualitative Analysis of Fertility Transition in Thailand." University of Michigan Population Studies Center, Research Report no. 83–44.

————. 1984. "Fertility Transition in Thailand: A Qualitative Analysis." *Population and Development Review* 10(2): 297–328.

Kuznets, Simon. 1966. *Modern Economic Growth: Rate, Structure, and Spread*. New Haven: Yale University Press.

Lee, Ronald D., and Rodolfo A. Bulatao. 1983. "The Demand for Children: A Critical Essay." In R. Bulatao and R. D. Lee, eds., *Determinants of Fertility in Developing Countries: A Summary of Knowledge*. New York: Academic Press.

Leibenstein, Harvey. 1957. *Economic Backwardness and Economic Growth*. New York: John Wiley.

————. 1974. "An Interpretation of the Economic Theory of Fertility: Promising Path or Blind Alley?" *Journal of Economic Literature* 12 (2) (June): 457–79.

Lerner, D. 1968. "Modernization, I—Social Aspects." In David L. Sills, ed., *International Encyclopedia of the Social Sciences* 10:386–95. New York: Macmillan.

Lesthaeghe, R. J., and H. J. Page. 1980. "The Post-Partum Non-Susceptible Period: Development and Application of Model Schedules." *Population Studies* 34:143–69.

Lindert, Peter H. 1980. "Child Costs and Economic Development." In Richard A. Easterlin, ed., *Population and Economic Change in Developing Countries*, 5–69. Chicago: Chicago University Press.

———. 1983. "The Changing Economic Costs and Benefits of Having Children." In R. Bulatao and R. D. Lee, eds., *Determinants of Fertility in Developing Countries: A Summary of Knowledge.* New York: Academic Press.

McClelland, Gary H. 1983. "Family Size Desires as Measures of Demand." In R. Bulatao and R. D. Lee, eds., *Determinants of Fertility in Developing Countries: A Summary of Knowledge.* New York: Academic Press.

McNicoll, Geoffrey. 1980. "Institutional Determinants of Fertility Change." *Population and Development Review* 6 (3): 441–62.

Maddala, G. S. 1983. *Limited-Dependent and Qualitative Variables in Econometrics.* Cambridge: Cambridge University Press.

Malenbaum, Wilfred. 1970. "Health and Productivity in Poor Areas." In H. E. Klarman, ed., *Empirical Studies in Health Economics,* 31–54. Baltimore: Johns Hopkins University Press.

Mauldin, W. Parker, and Robert J. Lapham. 1980. "Measuring the Impact of Family Planning Programs." Paper presented at the Seminar on the Use of Surveys for the Analysis of Family Planning Programmes, Bogotá, Colombia, October 28–31.

Mhloyi, Marvellous. 1984. "Fertility Determinants: A Comparative Study of Kenya and Lesotho." Ph.D. diss., University of Pennsylvania.

Michael, Robert T., and Robert J. Willis. 1976. "Contraception and Fertility: Household Production under Uncertainty." In Conference on Research in Income and Wealth, *Household Production and Consumption,* 27–94. New York: National Bureau of Economic Research.

Morawetz, David. 1977. *Twenty-five Years of Economic Development, 1950 to 1975.* Washington, D.C.: The World Bank.

Mueller, Eva, and Kathleen Short. 1983. "Effects of Income and Wealth on the Demand for Children." In R. Bulatao and R. D. Lee, eds., *Determinants of Fertility in Developing Countries: A Summary of Knowledge.* New York: Academic Press.

Nag, Moni. 1980. "How Modernization Can Also Increase Fertility." *Current Anthropology* 21 (5) (October): 27–36.

———. 1983. "Modernization Affects Fertility." *Populi* 10(1): 56–77.

Nortman, Dorothy L. 1978. "India's New Birth Rate Target: An Analysis." *Population and Development Review* 4 (2) (June): 277–312.

Operations Research Group. 1971. *Family Planning Practices in India.* Baroda: Ashok Printery.

Page, Hilary J., and Ron Lesthaeghe. 1981. *Child-Spacing in Tropical Africa: Traditions and Change.* London: Academic Press.

Pittenger, D. B. 1973. "An Exponential Model of Female Sterility." *Demography* 10:113–21.

Poston, Dudley L., and Katherine Trent. 1984. "Modernization and Childlessness in the Developing World." *Comparative Social Research* 7. Forthcoming.

Potter, Joseph E. 1983. "Effects of Societal and Community Institutions on Fertility." In R. Bulatao and R. D. Lee, eds., *Determinants of Fertility in Developing Countries: A Summary of Knowledge*. New York: Academic Press.

Retherford, Robert D. 1980. "Modeling Sudden and Rapid Fertility Decline." Working Paper no. 1. Honolulu: East-West Population Institute.

Retherford, Robert D., and James A. Palmore. 1983. "Diffusion Processes Affecting Fertility Regulation." In R. Bulatao and R. D. Lee, eds., *Determinants of Fertility in Developing Countries: A Summary of Knowledge*. New York: Academic Press.

Richards, Toni. 1983. "Statistical Studies of Aggregate Fertility Change: Time Series of Cross-Sections." In R. Bulatao and R. D. Lee, eds., *Determinants of Fertility in Developing Countries: A Summary of Knowledge*. New York; Academic Press.

Robinson, Warren C. 1983. "Economic Development and Population Control." *Journal of East Asian Affairs* 3 (2) (Fall–Winter): 442–54.

Rosovsky, Henry, and K. Ohkawa. 1961. "The Indigenous Components in the Modern Japanese Economy." *Economic Development and Cultural Change* 9 (April): 476–501.

Sauvy, A. 1961. *General Theory of Population*. New York: Basic Books.

Schultz, T. Paul. 1976. "Determinants of Fertility: A Micro-Economic Model of Choice." In Ansley J. Coale, ed., *Economic Factors in Population Growth*, 89–124. New York: Halsted Press.

———. 1981. *Economics of Population*. Reading, Mass.: Addison-Wesley Publishing Co.

Srinivasan, K., et al. 1972. *Family Planning Targets by States for India*. Bombay: International Institute for Population Studies.

Srinivasan, K., and S. Jejeebhoy. 1981. "Changes in Natural Fertility in India, 1959–1972." In K. Srinivasan and S. Mukerji, eds., *Dynamics of Population and Family Welfare*. Bombay: Himalaya Publishing House.

Srinivasan, K., P. H. Reddy, and K. N. M. Raju. 1977. *Changes over a Generation in Fertility Levels and Values in Karnataka*. Occasional Papers, Series no. 2. Bangalore: Population Centre Bangalore.

———. 1978. "One Generation to the Next: Changes in Fertility, Family Size Preferences, and Family Planning in an Indian State between 1951 and 1975." *Studies in Family Planning* 9:258–71.

Tabarrah, Riad B. 1971. "Toward a Theory of Demographic Development." *Economic Development and Cultural Change* 19 (2) (January): 257–77.

Titmuss, R. M. 1966. *Essays on the Welfare State*. London: Unwin University Press.

United Nations. 1961. *The Mysore Population Study*. New York: United Nations Department of Economic and Social Affairs.

———. 1965. *Population Bulletin of the United Nations*, no. 7:1963. New York: United Nations Department of Economic and Social Affairs.

————. 1966. *Report on the Family Planning Programme in India.* Report no. TAO/IND/48. United Nations.

————. 1969. *An Evaluation of the Family Planning Programme of the Government of India.* Report no. TAO/IND/50. New York: United Nations.

————. 1979. *Factors Affecting the Use and Non-Use of Contraception.* Population Studies no. 69. New York: United Nations.

————. 1981. *Variations in the Incidence of Knowledge and Use of Contraception: A Comparative Analysis of World Fertility Survey Results of Twenty Developing Countries.* New York: United Nations.

Wachter, Michael L. 1972. "Government Policy toward the Fertility of the Poor." Fels Discussion Paper no. 19. University of Pennsylvania, Philadelphia.

Willis, Robert J. 1974. "Economic Theory of Fertility Behavior." In T. W. Schultz, ed., *Economics of the Family.* Chicago: University of Chicago Press.

Wongboonsin, Kua. 1985. "Fertility Patterns and Their Determinants in Thailand, 1969–1979: Results from Cross-sectional and Longitudinal Studies." Ph.D. diss., University of Pennsylvania.

Name Index

Subject Index

Abortion: as contraceptive method, 46; knowledge and approval of, 51, 55, 70–72. *See also* Pregnancy wastage

Abstinence: as contraceptive method, 46; in Karnataka and Taiwan studies, 134, 137; in sub-Saharan Africa, 46; test of, as variable, 37

Access to fertility control. *See* Family planning programs, access to

Actual fertility, 35–36, 50, 101

Africa, and taboo on intercourse, 46

Age at first use of fertility control, 46–47

Age at marriage: as estimate of age at first use, 47; impact of, on fertility, 8, 19; test of, as variable in analysis, 37

Age of surviving child, as measure of length of use, 152

Age specific fertility schedule, tilt in, 141–43, 187

Age: impact of, on demand for children, 125, 187; and relation to fertility differentials, 141–43

Agriculture, impact of, on demand for children, 25

Andhra Pradesh, 149, 152–70

Approval of family planning, as measure of regulation costs, 150–51, 156, 160

Attitudes to fertility control. *See* Causation, direction of; Fertility control, attitudes toward

Bangalore Population Study, 123–24

Baroda Operations Research Group, 148–49

Bias, analysis of, in sample, 42, 45, 48–49, 52, 109–16, 156–57

Birth control. *See* Fertility control; Perfect contraceptive society

Birth interval: among regulators and nonregulators, 66; as variable in analysis, 36–41; assumptions about, 108–9; definition of, 54; estimation of, 47

Births. *See* Fertility

Births averted: approximation of, 43; as measure of conscious control, 8; in Karnataka, 131–32, 135; in Sri Lanka and Colombia, 79–80; in Taiwan, 135

Breastfeeding: as contraceptive method, 46; and impact on fertility, 7, 43, 62, 179

Breastfeeding, duration of: among regulators and nonregulators, 66; as approximation of postpartum infecundability, 37; as variable in analysis, 36–41; assumptions about, 108–9; definition of, 54; impact of education on, 92, 143, 146; in relation to education in Sri Lanka and Colombia, 91; significance of, in Sri Lanka and Colombia, 81

Causation, direction of: and effect of use on attitude, 51, 70–73, 151, 156, 166, 184; and wife's work status, 90

203

Easterlin, Richard
Ainley

The fertility
revolution

DATE DUE
